"This is a highly accessible introductory account of why we need curriculum-based professional learning and the changes needed, both structural and normative, in educators' practices and in different roles at all levels of school systems to transform its promise into day-to-day instruction reliably implemented with quality at scale. Much of what we have learned from learning science and the first-hand work of improving schools over the last 30 years is succinctly summarized in the pages of this book."

—Tony Bryk
Former President of the Carnegie Foundation
for the Advancement of Teaching

"The elements of curriculum-based professional learning encapsulate what school system leaders have long known: successful curriculum implementation and excellent teaching require an informed, multi-pronged approach. This book weaves together research and real-world evidence in an actionable manner, equipping stakeholders with valuable tools that will have a profound impact on the K–12 education space."

—Mike Magee
Former CEO, Chiefs for Change

"The adoption of high-quality instructional materials is one of the most promising developments of recent years. But even the best curricula don't teach themselves; only when educators have the chance to study materials at depth will this latest reform fulfill its potential. In this critically important book, James B. Short and Stephanie Hirsh offer a detailed guide for making it happen in the real world of schools and classrooms."

—Michael J. Petrilli
President, Thomas B. Fordham Institute

"Educators need and deserve high-quality instructional materials. But even the strongest, most educative curriculum is not enough on its own to support teachers and students. Through evidence, examples, and reflection, the *Elements* clearly document the key components of curriculum-based professional learning and how to build them. This book is essential reading for all educators, administrators, policymakers, and stakeholders."

—Eric Hirsch
Executive Director, EdReports

"This volume moves us past thinking of teachers as implementers of curriculum materials to thinking of teachers as learning engineers—professionals who apply their expertise and judgment to high-quality materials to drive learning gains. To demonstrate how we can make this transition, James B. Short and Stephanie Hirsh weave together engaging examples and research-proven, practical advice. This book is a must-have for anyone whose work touches teacher learning and instructional improvement."

—Heather Hill
Hazen-Nicoli Professor in Teacher Learning and Practice
Harvard Graduate School of Education

"This volume is one of the first of its kind to make a clear and compelling case for the connection between high-quality instructional materials and high-quality professional learning centered on those materials. This book can help with transforming the relevance and effectiveness of professional learning communities and reimagining traditional curriculum practices by moving from pacing guides and scripted curriculum to educative curriculum that supports and improves teacher practice. With compelling real-world examples from districts and the smart, eloquent *Elements* model, this book provides the theoretical framework, strategic direction, and practical guidance for meaningful and sustained improvement in the professional learning process for educators. Very smart connectors, such as the 'Changing Emphases' theme that runs throughout, will keep the reader engaged in seeing the transformational shifts that Short and Hirsh argue are needed."

—Segun Eubanks
Professor of Practice
Director of the Center for Educational Innovation and Improvement
University of Maryland College Park, College of Education

"At last: A call for professional learning for teachers infused with the deepest respect for the actual work of teaching. Short and Hirsh cut right to the chase, arguing that the most logical and intellectually engaging learning opportunities for teachers engage them individually and collectively in doing the work of the (ideally high-quality) curriculum from which they teach, 'mirroring' and 'modeling' the student curriculum and in the process supporting teachers to unpack and discuss the content, anticipate student thinking, and plan for how they will elicit and respond to diverse student ideas. Any other approach risks loitering on the fringes of the real work teachers do—interpreting demanding content and curriculum to meet the needs of individual students and communities. The 'essentials' are clearly laid out and illustrated with compelling examples from districts, making for an efficient read with a potentially huge payoff for teachers, principals, and district leaders."

—**Francesca Forzani**
Deputy Director at TeachingWorks

"We are teachers at heart, with 22 classroom years between us. Teachers deserve high-quality materials accompanied by high-quality professional learning, as *Transforming Teaching Through Curriculum-Based Professional Learning* suggests. Educators bring the *Elements* to life for students, and we are especially convinced that the Core Design Features—Curriculum, Transformative Learning, and Equity—play a critical role."

—**Melissa Loftus** and **Lori Sappington**
Podcast Hosts
Melissa and Lori Love Literacy
Podcast Powered by Great Minds

Transforming Teaching
Through Curriculum-Based
Professional Learning

This book is dedicated to two dear friends and colleagues whose seminal work on designing professional learning and implementing change in schools continues to impact all of us.

Susan Loucks-Horsley (1947–2000)

and

Shirley Hord (1929–2019)

Transforming Teaching Through Curriculum-Based Professional Learning

The Elements

James B. Short

Stephanie Hirsh

Foreword by Linda Darling-Hammond

A Joint Publication With Learning Forward

FOR INFORMATION:

Corwin

A SAGE Company

2455 Teller Road

Thousand Oaks, California 91320

(800) 233-9936

www.corwin.com

SAGE Publications Ltd.

1 Oliver's Yard

55 City Road

London EC1Y 1SP

United Kingdom

SAGE Publications India Pvt. Ltd.

B 1/I 1 Mohan Cooperative Industrial Area

Mathura Road, New Delhi 110 044

India

SAGE Publications Asia-Pacific Pte. Ltd.

18 Cross Street #10-10/11/12

China Square Central

Singapore 048423

President: Mike Soules

Vice President and
  Editorial Director: Monica Eckman

Program Director
  and Publisher: Dan Alpert

Senior Content Development
  Editor: Lucas Schleicher

Associate Content
  Development Editor: Mia Rodriguez

Editorial Assistant: Natalie Delpino

Production Editor: Tori Mirsadjadi

Copy Editor: Melinda Masson

Typesetter: C&M Digitals (P) Ltd.

Indexer: Integra

Cover Designer: Scott Van Atta

Interior Designer: Gail Buschman

Marketing Manager: Melissa Duclos

Printed in the United States of America

Library of Congress Cataloging-in-Publication Data

Names: Short, James B., (Curriculum instructor) author. | Hirsh, Stephanie, author.

Title: Transforming teaching through curriculum-based professional learning : the elements / James B. Short, Stephanie Hirsh ; Foreword by Linda Darling-Hammond ; A Joint Publication With Learning Forward.

Description: Thousand Oaks, California : Corwin, [2023] | Includes bibliographical references and index.

Identifiers: LCCN 2022015185 | ISBN 9781071886328 (paperback) | ISBN 9781071886311 (epub) | ISBN 9781071886304 (epub) | ISBN 9781071886298 (pdf)

Subjects: LCSH: Teachers—Training of. | Curriculum planning—Study and teaching. | Inquiry-based learning.

Classification: LCC LB1707 .S56 2023 | DDC 370.71/15—dc23/eng/20220622

LC record available at https://lccn.loc.gov/2022015185

This book is printed on acid-free paper.

22 23 24 25 26 10 9 8 7 6 5 4 3 2 1

Contents

Foreword

Unlike teachers of the past, whose job was configured as marching through a textbook with their students, today's teachers are being asked to teach an ever more diverse group of learners more challenging material in ways that result in deeper understanding and more equitable outcomes. Furthermore, knowledge is expanding rapidly and technologies are changing the nature of life and work daily. Many students entering school today will leave to work in jobs that do not yet exist, using knowledge that has not yet been discovered and technologies that have not yet been invented, facing complex problems our generation has been unable to solve. Students today need much more than simply to recall a canon of received knowledge. They need to be able to find, analyze, synthesize, evaluate, and apply knowledge to new ideas, answers, and solutions; communicate in multiple forms, use technologies, and collaborate with others; and become able to learn on their own throughout life.

The kind of teaching required to support contemporary learning goals in this context is very different from what was required when the goal was merely to "cover the curriculum" and "get through the book," enabling some students to succeed if they could and others to fail. In order to enable very diverse students to learn the higher-order skills once reserved for a tiny few, teachers need a range of new skills. They must understand content more deeply and flexibly; they must understand the science of learning—how children learn and develop in cultural contexts, generally and individually, within and across distinctive subject areas; they must develop teaching strategies that foster analysis and reasoning; and they must continually incorporate appropriate technologies into their teaching practice.

As these realities place new demands on schools, the pressing issue of how to help teachers accomplish such daunting goals is critical. The changes schools are expected to effectuate cannot be teacher-proofed and handed down from on high. Supporting teachers' learning in systematic ways is the linchpin to school transformation. It is in the classroom that the direct engagement between students and the content and processes of their learning occurs and can be most effectively leveraged. The strategic moves that teachers make—in selecting and orchestrating materials, activities, examples, and support—are the primary mediators of learning.

This insightful book by James B. Short and Stephanie Hirsh makes an important contribution to our collective learning by examining how curriculum frameworks and high-quality instructional materials can support teachers' actions in ways that motivate and support much deeper student learning for a much wider range of students. While high-quality instructional materials embedded in strong curriculum designs are a critical tool appreciated by teachers when they are available, they are not a "silver bullet" solution for better student outcomes. Instead, they are part of a more complex implementation process that relies on high-quality curriculum-based professional learning—something that is still relatively rare in the United States. The *Elements* provide a framework for system leaders, curriculum developers, and specialists in professional learning to address this challenge.

Whereas professional learning in many countries has long been grounded in a national or state curriculum, until recently in the United States, much professional learning has been focused either on how to use textbooks by marching through chapters focused on specific topics or on more general instructional principles that teachers seek to apply to their classrooms. It is only recently that we have seen more widespread efforts to design professional learning grounded in high-quality instructional materials aimed at higher-order thinking and performance skills associated with new curriculum standards.

A critical problem is that, for many teachers, the kind of teaching expected by these new standards differs from what they have taught in the past and from how they experienced learning themselves when they were students. This means a different type of professional learning is needed. Short and Hirsh provide a view of curriculum-based professional learning in which teachers immerse themselves in lessons as learners to experience student thinking. Because curriculum-based professional learning is anchored in the instructional materials teachers will use with their students, it provides teachers with opportunities to take on a learner perspective and experience the lessons and activities in high-quality instructional materials themselves to inform their curriculum planning. They then transition to planning that involves making decisions on how they will teach a lesson in ways that can meet the diverse needs of students and ensure the curriculum is culturally relevant.

This approach is hugely valuable and, based on prior research, likely to result in much greater success for students. In 2017, my colleagues at the Learning Policy Institute examined the studies on professional development that documented changes in teacher practice associated with significant gains in student achievement. We found that there were seven common features of these efforts. This book illustrates how all of these design features can be implemented as Core, Structural, or Functional Design *Elements* of curriculum-based professional learning. For example, in *Effective Teacher Professional Development,* my colleagues and I observed that such learning:

- **Is content focused**, developing teaching strategies associated with specific curriculum content. This book's Core Design *Elements* describe how the use of high-quality instructional materials can help build teachers' disciplinary content knowledge, pedagogical knowledge, and pedagogical content knowledge.

- **Incorporates active learning** in ways that directly engage teachers in designing and trying out teaching strategies, providing them an opportunity to engage in the same style of learning they are designing for their students. In its discussion of Functional Design *Elements*, this book describes how adult learners can be actively engaged in experiencing the instructional approaches embedded in high-quality curriculum materials, thus mirroring active teacher learning on the learning teachers are expected to create for students in classrooms. The Learning Designs *Element* prioritizes inquiry-based learning experiences for teachers that model sense-making strategies teachers will use with students.

- **Supports collaboration** by creating space for teachers to share ideas and collaborate in their learning, often in job-embedded contexts. As part of the Structural Design *Elements*, the authors elevate the importance of collaboration among teachers who are using the same instructional materials to create a community of practice that can grow and learn together.

- **Uses models of effective practice** by providing curricular models and modeling of instruction that offer teachers a clear vision of what best practices look like. These may include lesson plans, unit plans, sample student work, observations of peer teachers, and video or written cases of teaching. The authors note that all these aspects of modeling are part of a successful launch and can be revisited through professional learning community (PLC) cycles and deeper support throughout the school year. In the book's section on Functional Design *Elements*, the authors describe how curriculum-based professional learning can support teachers in analyzing the sample lessons and classroom videos of students engaged in learning with the materials.

- **Provides coaching and expert support** that offers expertise about content and evidence-based practices, focused directly on teachers' individual needs. These are incorporated in the Models *Element*, with an emphasis on choosing the appropriate model for the intended outcome.

- **Offers feedback and reflection opportunities** for teachers to think about, receive input on, and make changes to their practice. As a Functional Design *Element*, the authors define such opportunities as facilitated time when teachers think about new instructional materials, receive input on how best to use them, examine student work and assessment data, and make changes to instructional practice in response.

- **Is of sustained duration**, providing teachers with adequate time to learn, practice, implement, and reflect upon new strategies that facilitate changes in their practice. This is a key part of the Structural Design *Elements* and is carried through in the authors' discussions of leadership, resources, and coherence.

The final chapter of the book explains how to put the *Elements* into action, with recommendations for teachers, school-based coaches, professional learning providers, curriculum developers, and district curriculum coordinators, as well as school and system leaders. These recommendations provide guidance for creating better professional learning systems and pathways for teachers and leaders in ways that help translate the big ideas of curriculum-based professional learning into the day-to-day actions that can transform teaching.

It is exciting to look forward to a day when we may have systems of support for learning that bring together high-quality curriculum resources and expert teachers in a virtuous cycle of improved instruction on behalf of all students. Some years ago, when my colleagues and I were studying five leading nations for our book *Empowered Educators*, we noted that "Producing highly skilled and committed teachers is not the work of a single innovative school or the aggregation of heroic individuals who succeed against the odds. In high-performing countries, the opportunities for teachers to learn sophisticated practices and continue to improve are embedded systemically in education policies and practices." This book points the way toward a coherent set of policies, tools, and practices designed that educational systems can use to ensure quality teaching in all communities. I trust there are many who will benefit from its wisdom.

—Linda Darling-Hammond

Acknowledgments

Curriculum-based professional learning and many of the related ideas addressed in this book have been influenced by countless educators who have provided leadership, thought partnership, and technical assistance to improve its application in practice and make a difference for educators and students. We are grateful to them for the important contributions they have made to the field and the important work many continue to do each day. Without their long-term commitment to these efforts in the educational field, we would not be writing this book. We recognize their contributions and cite their scholarship throughout the book as well as our efforts to continue to make compelling and accessible the ideas they advocate and advance.

We are fortunate to have worked with many of the individuals cited in the book. First and foremost are the late Susan Loucks-Horsley and Shirley Hord, who played seminal roles in our development as professional learning educators, as well as how we approach curriculum-based professional learning. We also learned from other visionary leaders in the field of professional learning, including Dennis Sparks, Linda Darling-Hammond, Susan Mundry, Kathy DiRanna, Kathy Stiles, and Jody Bintz. Jim acknowledges others with meaningful influence on his development, including Rodger Bybee, Jo Topps, Kate McNeill, Renee Affolter, and Dora Kastel. Stephanie acknowledges those who played a similar role in her development as a professional learning leader, including Gerald Ponder, Hayes Mizell, Joellen Killion, Sandra Alberti, and Tracy Crow. Most important are the individuals who lead this work on a daily basis in technical assistance and intermediary organizations, professional associations, and school systems who are the unsung heroes of curriculum-based professional learning, and we salute their efforts. We also deeply appreciate the researchers who continue to study this work and conduct research that is critical to the field.

Standards-based reform efforts increased the interest and demand for high-quality instructional materials and more explicit direction for curriculum-based professional learning. These efforts leading to state adoptions of academic, teaching, and leadership standards established a need for more effective and focused professional learning. Learning

Forward (formerly National Staff Development Council) has pioneered efforts in the development, dissemination, and adoption of professional learning standards for more than three decades, demonstrating how such standards could be used to improve practice and outcomes for students. Linda Darling-Hammond and colleagues at the Learning Policy Institute have documented the features of effective professional learning, and more recently Student Achievement Partners' contribution of *Principles for High-Quality, Standards-Aligned Professional Learning* elevated these research-based nonnegotiables. The professional development design framework developed by Susan Loucks-Horsley and colleagues provides a process for designing professional learning that greatly influenced the development of the *Elements* for curriculum-based professional learning.

We acknowledge the grantees in the Leadership and Teaching to Advance Learning portfolio at Carnegie Corporation of New York for their contributions to the *Elements* framework including the exemplar stories showcased throughout the book, as well as for elevating the importance of curriculum-based professional learning in their work. These organizations include Achievement Network, EdReports, EL Education, Illustrative Mathematics, Instruction Partners, Leading Educators, Learning Forward, New Teacher Center, OpenSciEd, Student Achievement Partners, Teaching Lab, TNTP, and WestEd. We recognize the schools and systems committed to this work and their willingness to share their learning including Baltimore City Public Schools (MD), Boston Public Schools (MA), Caldwell Parish School District (LA), Charlotte-Mecklenburg Schools (NC), District of Columbia Public Schools (DC), Kansas City Public Schools (MO), Lafayette Parish School System (LA), Sullivan County Schools (TN), and Sunnyside Unified School District (AZ). We especially want to thank the educators who shared their stories with us, including Amy Bailey, Dana Carter, Valery Dragon, Marianne Dunne, Sarah Johnson, Brian Kingsley, Janise Lane, Robin McClellan, Kate McNeill, Dianna Newman, Victoria Paredes, Max Ray-Riek, Roselynn Rodriguez, Melody Salcido, and HaMy Vu.

This book began as a challenge paper published by Carnegie Corporation of New York. The ideas within it were shaped by the organizations and individuals identified above. In addition, we want to thank Kathleen Carroll, editor extraordinaire, who translated the foundational paper into compelling narrative and increased the accessibility and interest to a broader audience, and James McKibben, the designer who converted the early draft and concepts into compelling pictography. The report was produced under the leadership of the Corporation's LaVerne Srinivasan, Vice President, National Program and Program Director, Education; Julia Weede, Chief Communications and Digital Strategies

Officer; Kelly Devine, Director, Content and Publications; Debra Wexler, Communications Officer; and Daniel Kitae Um, Principal Design Director. Copy editing was conducted by Amy Mazzariello.

We are thankful for the skillful editors and designers from Corwin, including first and foremost Dan Alpert, whose thought-provoking support improved the draft of each chapter. We also extend appreciation to Learning Forward and Tracy Crow, Chief Strategy Officer, for including our book in the Learning Forward Book Club.

This project began in the fall of 2019 with a convening hosted by Carnegie Corporation of New York that included twenty grantee organizations and some of their school and district partners. Six months later, the COVID-19 pandemic was upon us and remained for almost two years. The elements of curriculum-based professional learning were developed and refined during this historic time in our country. After we completed the challenge paper, which was published by the Corporation in late 2020, schools and systems continued to face challenges resulting from the pandemic. We listened and learned about new ways of supporting teachers through remote and hybrid learning environments. We are grateful for the educators who continued to maintain a focus on the importance of high-quality instructional materials and curriculum-based professional learning during these difficult times. We hope this book provides a framework that helps schools and systems continue improvement efforts that result in better outcomes for all students.

Finally, we thank our families for their patience and support. Without their encouragement while writing this book as we all learned to work from home, none of this would be possible.

About the Authors

James B. Short is a former science teacher who taught high school biology for ten years using research-based instructional materials. He has been involved in education for over thirty years with an ongoing focus on the role of curriculum and professional learning in teacher development. At BSCS Science Learning, he directed a national science curriculum and implementation center and led the development of the National Academy for Curriculum Leadership, working with district leadership teams around the country on the selection, adoption, and implementation of high-quality instructional materials. The three-year academy in curriculum leadership provided tools and processes for analyzing curricula and designing professional learning to support implementation. In Denver Public Schools he led the redesign of the K–12 science program with the adoption and district-wide implementation of new inquiry-based curricula. At the American Museum of Natural History in New York City, he was the founding director of the Gottesman Center for Science Teaching and Learning. He led the American Museum's efforts to strengthen science education programs at museums, nonprofit organizations, schools, and systems, including the New York City Department of Education. He oversaw the design and implementation of the Urban Advantage initiative in New York City, a partnership program in nearly half of the city's middle schools, supporting inquiry-based learning and teaching. He was on the faculty of the American Museum's master of arts in teaching program, a first-of-its-kind urban teacher residency program for developing certified earth science teachers, and taught courses in curriculum and teaching. More recently, he taught science education courses in the midcareer doctoral program in educational leadership at the University of Pennsylvania Graduate School of Education.

James is currently the program director for Leadership and Teaching to Advance Learning in the education program at Carnegie Corporation of New York. His work at the foundation focuses on building capacity of teachers, principals, and system leaders to implement college- and career-ready standards in language arts and reading, mathematics, and science. The portfolio invests in the development of high-quality instructional materials and curriculum-based professional learning for teachers and instructional leaders. Building on the foundation's support for new science standards, the Corporation launched OpenSciEd in 2018 partnering with other foundations and supporting ten states to improve the supply of and demand for high-quality science instructional materials and curriculum-based professional learning. In 2020, James coauthored with Stephanie Hirsh *The Elements: Transforming Teaching Through Curriculum-Based Professional Learning.*

James earned a bachelor's degree in biology from Rhodes College, a master's in science education from Peabody College for Teachers at Vanderbilt University, and a doctorate in education with a focus on curriculum and instruction from Teachers College at Columbia University. He can be reached at jbs@carnegie.org.

Stephanie Hirsh is the former executive director of Learning Forward, a position she held for over a decade. Before her appointment as executive director, she served the association as deputy executive director for eighteen years. During her tenure she coauthored more than a dozen books, published more than one hundred articles, lectured internationally, and consulted with policy and decision makers broadly. She led the publication of the first three editions of *Standards for Professional Learning* as well as federal and state policies that leveraged them for more than three decades. Her advocacy, writing, and consulting efforts focused on building systems of professional learning that ensured high levels of learning and performance for all educators and students. Prior to her work with Learning Forward, she served as a teacher, central office administrator, and three-term school board member in the Richardson Independent School District (TX). Today she consults with foundations, organizations, education startups, and universities focused on issues of capacity building, equity, curriculum, and professional learning. Recent clients include Carnegie Corporation of New York, Chicago Public Schools, Learning Forward, National Center for Teacher Residencies, University of Maryland College of Education, and University of Texas College of Education.

Selected recent books and reports include *Preparing Day-One Ready Teachers* (2021), coauthored with Tabitha Grossman; *The Learning Principal: Becoming a Learning Leader* (2020), coauthored with Frederick Brown and Kay Psencik; *The Elements: Transforming Teaching Through Curriculum-Based Professional Learning* (2020), co-authored with James B. Short; *Becoming a Learning Team* (2017), coauthored with Tracy Crow; and *A School Board Guide to Leading Successful Schools* (2013), co-authored with Anne Foster.

Stephanie serves on advisory boards for Center for Public Research and Leadership at Columbia Law School, EdCuration, edsUP, Learning Forward, University of Kansas Center for Research on Learning's IES-funded research grant, University of Texas College of Education, and Dallas-area nonprofits. Stephanie has been recognized by the University of North Texas, Texas Association of School Boards, Texas Staff Development Council, Richardson Independent School District, Junior Achievement, and Kappa Delta Pi for her scholarship, volunteerism, and leadership. She earned her doctorate and master's in education from the University of North Texas and her bachelor of science from the University of Texas at Austin. She can be reached at stephanie@hirshholdings.com.

Introduction

Elements are the fundamental building blocks for all matter in the world. Elements are also the building blocks of what matters most. Using high-quality instructional materials well matters for students. Effective professional learning to support curriculum implementation matters for teachers. What are the elements of curriculum-based professional learning—the subject matter of this book—that produce desired outcomes for teachers and students? This book is meant to answer this question by focusing on the design features and enabling conditions that are elemental and matter most for curriculum-based professional learning.

Curriculum Implementation as Learning

For too long and in too many cases, investments in professional learning have failed to achieve their intended outcomes. Many educational leaders and policymakers have lost hope and looked for other solutions to support students. But as studies consistently show,[1] the greatest indicator of a student's success is the quality of teaching experienced every day. Any plan for better serving students must work for teachers and meet their needs too. There is no simple or silver-bullet solution. Fortunately, in the last several years, emerging research[2] has demonstrated the value of providing teachers with high-quality educative instructional materials. Upon further examination, we learn that high-quality curricula alone are not the answer. Lacking support and pressure to use these types of curricula well and in ways they were intended, teachers can ignore, adapt, or attempt implementation with mixed outcomes. As a result, both high-quality instructional materials and curriculum-based professional learning will position schools and systems to achieve their dual goals of equity and excellence.

Simply introducing a new curriculum is unlikely to change teacher practices. Research shows that curriculum reform is accomplished through a systemic approach that requires new instructional materials and new ways of using them.[3] Putting curriculum reforms into practice is a difficult and demanding process that requires a vision for instructional reform, support for change, collaboration among teachers to learn, and leadership at multiple levels. Reform-oriented "educative" instructional materials incorporate contemporary research on how students learn content and challenge teachers to think differently about learning and teaching disciplinary content knowledge. Teachers who are unfamiliar with such curricula want relevant professional learning to help them implement educative instructional materials effectively.

Educative instructional materials challenge teachers to think differently about learning and teaching content. Instead of a textbook that provides only "what to teach," these instructional materials also provide support for "how to teach." Because incorporating support for teaching into instructional materials makes them different and educative for both student and teacher learning, most teachers benefit from a rich form of ongoing professional learning that helps them learn how to use such materials effectively. This type of professional learning is grounded in immersive learning experiences for teachers where they experience as learners the new instructional materials in ways that mirror their intended use with students.

A Vision for Improvement

High-performing educational systems recognize the importance of strong instructional support systems to achieve equity for all students. They adopt compelling instructional visions including college-and career-ready standards and provide teachers with educative instructional materials and effective professional learning focused on transforming their beliefs and practices relevant to teaching and learning. They develop a local improvement infrastructure that includes resources and people (including the expertise of both administrators and teachers as well as intermediary organizations) that are positioned to improve the system. To obtain access to these resources and provide the pressure and support for sustained change, many partner with nonprofit organizations with expertise in professional learning, school improvement, instructional design, disciplinary content, and curriculum development.

How are high-performing systems, charters, and schools able to accomplish such heavy lifting? To learn what they have in common, in 2019 Carnegie Corporation of New York[4] invited a group of grantees who are leading professional learning providers and curriculum developers to bring school system partners to a convening that revealed the shared characteristics of these transformations. We wanted to learn the key components of curriculum-based professional learning. Over the course of two days and through follow-up conversations and interviews as well as a deep dive into the literature and research on curriculum implementation and professional learning, we asked questions, listened closely, and learned.

What Is Curriculum-Based Professional Learning?

This work resulted in a core set of research-based actions, approaches, and enabling conditions that effective schools and systems have put in place to reinforce and amplify the power of high-quality curriculum and skillful teaching. We call these the *Elements of curriculum-based professional learning*, or simply the *Elements*.

Curriculum-based professional learning focuses primarily on the implementation of high-quality instructional materials. Curriculum-based professional learning is anchored in the instructional materials teachers will use with their students. High-quality educative curriculum materials address both the content and the pedagogy necessary for effective instruction; curriculum-based professional learning offers the immediate and sustained support for successful implementation.

The *Elements* encompass actions big and small, from purposefully planning an immersive learning experience to orient teachers to using new instructional materials to mapping a three-year plan for ongoing support to sustain curriculum implementation efforts. The *Elements* offer a framework for practitioners looking to undertake this work. They also serve as a call to action. This powerful approach to curriculum reform and professional learning knits together two influential aspects of a child's education: teachers' skillfulness and the quality of the instructional materials teachers use to support student learning. By reshaping current practices with the *Elements* as a guide, we can help teachers further develop the skills, knowledge, and understanding they need to achieve their goals of equity and excellence for all students.

Purpose of the Book

The book is intended to help educators gain new knowledge regarding the importance of curriculum-based professional learning as well as the related field of high-quality educative instructional materials. We hope this information will promote deeper understanding and appreciation of the *Elements* of curriculum-based professional learning. Throughout the book we help readers examine and analyze how curriculum-based professional learning differs from traditional professional learning and the key shifts in practice it demands. A deeper understanding of the *Elements* of effective curriculum-based professional learning positions readers to critique adult learning experiences through a new lens and consider changes for the future. And finally, we offer readers role-related responsibilities and next actions for consideration.

We wrote this book during the COVID-19 pandemic, a time of great challenge as well as learning for the United States. While all students faced obstacles, those already underserved faced even more. Many organizations including the Learning Policy Institute called for an evidence-based, equity-centered approach for strengthening outcomes for all students.[5] School systems were encouraged to focus on the instructional core—the set of key relationships among teacher, student, and instructional materials that propel student learning day to day and fuel improvement over time. Expanded definitions of the instructional core included parents and caregivers as key partners in student learning.[6] The presence and availability of high-quality, tech-enabled instructional materials made these priorities easier to address. Innovative solutions were tested, and practices adjusted based on findings. Some of these learnings from the pandemic apply to the subject of this book—curriculum-based professional learning—which we identify and address throughout the chapters.

What We Know About Professional Learning

- Most professional development rarely achieves substantial positive impacts on teacher performance or student outcomes.[7]

- A broad gap exists between the short-term, isolated experiences that typify professional development and the ongoing, content-focused, job-embedded professional learning that can help teachers and their students excel.[8]

- Even when learning is focused on a particular content area, it tends to be short-lived, with most teachers participating in no more than sixteen hours of activities—on the order of a seminar or two—in a year.[9]

- Just 7 percent of the nation's elementary school reading teachers use at least one standards-aligned instructional tool in classroom instruction.[10]

- More than half of U.S. teachers craft curriculum for their students, either by borrowing from multiple sources or by creating their own materials.[11]

- Using better instructional materials boosts student outcomes just as much as having a better teacher at the front of the room.[12]

- When teachers participated in curriculum-based professional learning, their students' test scores improved by 9 percent of a standard deviation—about the same effect caused by replacing an average teacher with a top performer or reducing class size by 15 percent.[13]

- See Chapter 1 to learn more about the implications of this research.

Values Shared by the Authors

We wrote this book because of concerns and values we share. We are concerned that too little progress has been made in the field of professional learning in the last decade. And yet we see tremendous promise that developments in the specific field of high-quality instructional materials and curriculum-based professional learning can accelerate K–12 education toward the goals we want for educators and students. Supporting teachers to use new curriculum needs to be less about "training" and more about "learning." We believe in the simple idea that teachers will benefit most when their learning is anchored in the instructional materials they use with students, and they experience the inquiry-based learning we expect them to provide for their students. We believe our greatest opportunity to achieve equity is through teachers who are empowered with and prepared to help all students achieve challenging college- and career-ready standards. Finally, we believe in the power of leadership, instructional vision, and commitment to make curriculum-based professional learning a reality for more educators.

Our vision of professional learning uses curriculum as both a lever and a guide, helping link teachers' actions and ideas to new standards in a concrete, focused way. Done right, curriculum-based professional learning can close the gap between the experiences we provide teachers and those we want them to provide students. Given the challenges teachers and students faced as they learned to adapt to remote instructional platforms, such learning is especially crucial to their success. We have the opportunity to transform teaching by providing teachers with high-quality, standards-aligned instructional materials and supporting them with curriculum-based professional learning.

The Audience for This Book

The book is written for K–12 educators and stakeholders. Teachers and school-based coaches may use this book to deepen their understanding of the essential components of successful curriculum implementation. They may use it to guide their own planning and learning agenda as well as the support they may seek for successful implementation. School systems as well as experts in curriculum development and professional learning coordinators, consultants, and administrators are often the individuals with the greatest responsibility for reviewing, designing, and implementing curriculum-based professional learning with educators. Each detail of this book can guide these actions. Principals and school system leaders with authority and responsibility will want to focus on the last three *Elements* or essentials for they offer the conditions for achieving the potential impact of the investment in curriculum-based professional learning. Oversight responsibility for the other ten *Elements* is also a key responsibility, and suggestions for managing it are embedded throughout the book. The final chapter elaborates on the roles and responsibilities as well as ways in which to introduce the *Elements* into a school or system. Of course, other stakeholders can benefit from reading the book and considering implications for their work with educators including faculty in teacher preparation programs, state agency policy and program administrators, technical assistance providers, foundations, and other policymakers including local school board members.

Key Definitions

This book uses several terms that are not always commonly shared by the education field. We offer the following definitions to help readers understand our perspective and approach to this important endeavor.

- A **curriculum** is the design teachers use to plan, implement, and assess the learning outcomes for students.

- A **high-quality curriculum** includes standards-aligned instructional materials that teachers use, as well as resources that states and districts provide to support instruction, such as state standards, frameworks, scope and sequences, district instructional guidance, and interim assessments.

- Instructional materials and curriculum materials refer to the concrete resources that teachers use to provide standards-aligned learning experiences for students, as well as those that offer support and guidance for teachers on how to teach the materials.

- High-quality instructional materials and curriculum materials include specific learning goals and sets of detailed lessons and unit plans aligned to content standards, student-centered approaches to inquiry-based learning, research-based teaching strategies, teacher support materials, and embedded formative assessments to effectively help teachers implement coherent instructional units and courses that are organized around a clear scope and sequence.

- When high-quality instructional materials and curriculum materials support both student and teacher learning, they are considered educative curriculum materials.

Organization of the Book

We follow a similar pattern in each chapter. We begin and end with reflective questions intended to focus readers on the status of their current efforts related to curriculum implementation and curriculum-based professional learning. These questions may also serve as a status check as well as guidance for next steps. The narrative of each chapter begins as well as ends with an actual story about curriculum implementation in an American school system. These stories are meant to illustrate what the *Elements* can look like in action. Through a diversity of stories including geography, subjects, and grade levels, we hope all readers find components that resonate and motivate toward the importance of this work. Following each story is a thorough analysis of one or more *Elements* including attention to definitions, evidence, research, and distinctions from more traditional professional development. Reflection questions strategically placed within each chapter are intended to promote further consideration and application.

The first three chapters of the book introduce the reader to curriculum-based professional learning, the shifts required in practice, and an overview of the *Elements*. Most of the *Elements* focus on design features addressing the purpose and substance of curriculum-based professional learning. Design features are intended to guide designers, facilitators, and decision makers responsible for planning and implementing curriculum-based professional learning that supports teachers as they use high-quality instructional materials. These *Elements* are organized into three key components:

- Core Design features,

- Structural Design features, and

- Functional Design features.

Chapter 4 describes three Core Design features focused on the purposes of curriculum-based professional learning. Chapter 5 describes three Structural Design features that are the parameters or settings for professional learning. And Chapter 6 describes four Functional Design features that inform how teachers experience curriculum-based professional learning. Chapter 7 describes the last three *Elements* or **Essentials** that act as enabling conditions and define specific expectations of system leaders, principals, and teachers for implementing curriculum-based professional learning. Chapter 8 focuses on putting the *Elements* into action and describes the roles and responsibilities of teachers and school-based coaches; professional learning providers, curriculum developers, and district curriculum coordinators; and system and school leaders.

How to Use This Book

We can imagine educators using this book for independent learning or group-organized learning. We can see educators engaging in study groups to consider its ideas and whether to enact them. We can imagine its usefulness in leadership preparation programs as well as certifications for master teachers, instructional coaches, curriculum designers, and professional learning facilitators. We hope that educators will see it as a valuable resource that they will return to often when different situations surface that they recall are discussed within this text. We hope foundations and policymakers find it useful in launching new conversations regarding their investments and policies that can be leveraged to advance the ideas we present. And finally, we hope that researchers find components worthy of additional study and ultimately contribute new understandings to an expanded and well-documented field of curriculum-based professional learning.

Closing Thoughts

Teachers' jobs are changing in real time. Our commitment to equity and excellence, teachers, and students in all schools has never been more important. Over the past decade, college- and career-ready standards have dramatically shifted our expectations for student learning. It's no longer enough to raise a hand and give the right answer. Instead, we want students to wrestle with complex problems, collaborate with one another, and investigate and apply information in creative ways.

This is not how most teachers learned when they were in school. It is not how most teacher preparation programs develop adults to lead a classroom. And it looks nothing like the seminars that dominate teachers' professional development experiences. Most often, the emphasis is on creative lesson planning and keeping students engaged. While that can contribute to better teaching, it keeps the focus on the adult in the room. That focus needs to change.

School board members, parents, education stakeholders, and all educators have a vested interest in the success of all students. And many witnessed throughout the pandemic one thing that is clearly supported by research: curriculum has a direct impact on student engagement and learning. The instructional materials that teachers use with their students can dramatically accelerate or hamper learning. Equally important is the way in which teachers use curriculum including the involvement of families and caregivers to support learning. Curriculum-based professional learning presents a unique opportunity to enhance the efforts of hardworking teachers: provide them with strong, high-quality, standards-aligned curriculum and make sure they know how to take advantage of everything it has to offer.

This book identifies and describes the *Elements* of effective curriculum-based professional learning, including how these *Elements* are being used to positively affect schools across the country. And it challenges school and system leaders, curriculum developers, and all specialists in professional learning to apply them. Teachers deserve the highest-quality professional learning to support the implementation of new instructional materials and high-quality curriculum. The *Elements of curriculum-based professional learning* provide essential guidance for transforming teaching and student learning.

A Transformative Approach to Teacher Learning

1

///

Where are you now?

- I am wondering what is meant by a transformative approach to teacher learning.

- I am curious about the relationship between curriculum reform and classroom teaching.

- I am seeking ways to improve classroom instruction and outcomes for students.

- I am committed to using research and best practices to benefit both teachers and students.

A "Strange Transition"

Victoria Paredes's tenth-grade geometry classroom is a busy, noisy place. Teenagers cluster in small groups, chattering in English and Spanish as they swap hypotheses and use clues to find the diameter of a circle. Right or wrong, they share their answers to probe and master the day's learning objective.

All this activity is part of a new problem-based curriculum at Desert View High School in Tucson, Arizona, where Paredes has taught for seven years. The *Illustrative Mathematics* curriculum emphasizes mathematical thinking and student discourse to promote active learning. The lessons look nothing like the traditional lectures of years past. Instead, they prompt the sort of complex, rigorous inquiry that educators envisioned when setting new college- and career-ready standards for student achievement.

This type of inquiry-based instructional approach can be energizing for teachers and students alike. Paredes beamed as she recalled the day her students figured out the inscribed angle theorem before it was formally introduced—an astonishing achievement at a school where just one in five students had passed a statewide math test the year before. On end-of-year surveys, her students wrote that the class "felt awesome" and that they "had a major say" in their learning. One student wrote, "We didn't have the answers given to us, and we actually had to learn." Another said, "The way you teach—the way you do not help solve problems—has helped me. I like math."

But lessons like Paredes's are not easy to adopt. Teaching this type of curriculum, where students' questions build on each other in unexpected ways, requires a different approach to planning and a reframing of the teacher's role. As she worked to implement this new approach, Paredes met regularly with a skilled mentor and a small group of teachers from Sunnyside Unified School District to dissect and rehearse upcoming lessons. "We would go over a whole lesson from top to bottom and really dive deep," she said, discussing what moments were most important, what questions were most likely to arise, and how to push students' thinking so that they would master a rigorous learning goal.

"I never stopped being surprised, pleasantly surprised, by my students," she said. "But the one difficult thing about implementing this is you have to be really intentional every single day in the classroom. . . . It's not just instruction, instruction, instruction. . . . You have to anticipate—if a kid says this, how am I going to respond, or how am I going to ask another kid to say this? So it's a lot less me talking, but it's a lot more in facilitation. It's a strange transition."

From Stand-and-Deliver to Inquiry-Based Learning

Teachers' jobs are changing in real time. Over the past decade, college- and career-ready academic standards, along with the latest education research, have dramatically shifted our expectations for student learning. Just getting the right answer is not enough. Students need strategies to work together and apply information to solve problems.

In classrooms responding to these changes, teachers facilitate while students do most of the talking. Learning is relevant and joyful, rooted in exploration and debate. Classes are unpredictable and challenging—especially for the adult circulating throughout the room or monitoring the message board, keeping the discussion on pace to achieve the goal for the day's lesson. School closures concerning public health issues related to the COVID-19 pandemic have only added to the challenge, as students and teachers were required to adopt new modes of communication and sophisticated technological tools for remote learning.

This is not how most teachers learned when they were in school. It is not how most teacher preparation programs develop adults to lead a classroom. And it looks nothing like the seminars that dominate teachers' professional development experiences that keep the focus on what the teacher can do rather than what the student will do. Most often, the emphasis is on creative lesson planning and keeping students engaged—a misguided update to traditional stand-and-deliver instruction. While such models of professional development provide teachers with new ideas about teaching, they keep the focus on the adult in the classroom.

The focus needs to change. And teachers like Paredes are looking to make the switch—to bridge the gap between their experiences as young learners and novice teachers and current expectations for teaching and learning. Most teachers have never experienced the sort of inquiry-based learning we expect them to provide for their students. How can we help them make this "strange transition" and keep pace with new goals for academic success?

Reflect on this:

1. Think back to your own K–12 experiences. How did you learn?

2. How would you describe the teaching methodologies that your teachers applied?

3. To what do you attribute the need for change?

Defining Our Terminology

This work begins by establishing a clear understanding of what we mean by curriculum and instructional materials. A *curriculum* is the design teachers use to plan, implement, and assess the learning outcomes for students. A *high-quality curriculum* includes standards-aligned instructional materials that teachers use, as well as resources that states and districts provide to support instruction, such as state standards, frameworks, scope and sequences, district instructional guidance, and interim assessments. The terms *instructional materials* and *curriculum materials* refer to the concrete resources that teachers use to provide standards-aligned learning experiences for students, as well as those that offer support and guidance for teachers on how to teach the materials. When we refer to *high-quality instructional materials* and *high-quality curriculum materials*, we mean those that include specific learning goals and sets of detailed lessons and unit plans aligned to content standards, student-centered approaches to inquiry-based learning, research-based teaching strategies, teacher support materials, and embedded formative assessments to effectively help teachers implement coherent instructional units and courses that are organized around a clear scope and sequence. Finally, when high-quality instructional and curriculum materials support both student and teacher learning, they are considered *educative curriculum materials*.

Instructional and Curriculum Materials Matter

Successful classroom teaching transformation can be accomplished using a systemic approach that begins by asking educators to select and adopt new instructional materials and then learn effective ways of using them.

Putting innovative curriculum into practice is a difficult and demanding implementation process that requires

- a shared vision of learning and teaching,

- support for change,

- collaboration among teachers to learn, and

- leadership at multiple levels.

High-quality instructional materials incorporate contemporary research on adult and student learning and challenge teachers to think differently about learning and teaching disciplinary content knowledge. Instead of providing only what to teach, these instructional materials must also provide support for instructional activities and research-backed teaching methods. However, due to a lack of familiarity with these types of instructional materials as well as the standards they support, teachers stand to benefit from relevant, ongoing professional learning that can help them implement these innovative materials effectively.

As a result of the substantial changes in practice that may be required to implement high-quality curricula, many teachers require shifts in their knowledge and beliefs about effective teaching and learning strategies. For these shifts to take place, teachers need to experience transformative professional learning that challenges their beliefs about and understanding of content, teaching practices, and contemporary views of learning.

Professional Learning Matters Too

An essential premise of this book is that teachers can strive to improve student learning through selecting and implementing high-quality instructional materials. The selection and use of high-quality curricula can be a critical "point of entry" for reforming the educational system. In today's education environment, teachers have varying degrees of responsibility for selection of instructional materials. Although a growing number of schools and systems use third-party reviews by educators of instructional materials to inform their decisions, in other settings teachers are encouraged and responsible for creating curriculum themselves. While such creativity is admirable, we know that not all materials are created equal.

High-quality instructional materials involve more than a textbook for students. Teachers and students alike benefit from materials that provide content for the students as well as an instructional approach to learning and teaching. Instructional materials that provide both are "educative curriculum materials" and do not resemble traditional textbooks and teachers' editions. Consider this: it is not uncommon to find in educative materials twenty-five pages or more to support teacher planning and decision making in approaching one lesson in student materials. Admittedly, many teachers are unaccustomed to this level of detailed preparation—all the more reason to provide professional learning experiences designed to support the selection and implementation of new instructional materials, to help inform teachers of useful criteria for making their selection, and to provide them with effective strategies for using those materials.

Professional learning experiences designed to support the implementation of new instructional materials incorporate several principles. The most important of these is that adult learning experiences mirror those of students; in other words, effective professional learning should include instructional methods that not only promote learning for adults but also mirror the methods to be used with students. High-quality instructional materials designed to increase student learning convey a view of teaching largely as a process of provoking students to think, supporting them as they work, and guiding them along productive paths to reach the intended learning outcomes. How are teachers—who are unaccustomed to this approach to learning and teaching—supposed to learn the strategies and pedagogical content knowledge necessary to effectively implement instructional materials that have these goals? We suggest that the professional learning experiences for teachers model the instructional approaches intended with students by becoming the strategy for how teachers learn to implement new instructional materials.

High-quality instructional materials or educative curriculum materials designed for college- and career-ready standards challenge teachers to think differently about learning and teaching. Instead of a textbook that provides only "what to teach," these instructional materials also provide support for "how to teach."

Curriculum-Based Professional Learning

Professional learning that focuses on the implementation of high-quality instructional materials is referred to as curriculum-based professional learning. It invites teachers to participate in the same sort of rich, inquiry-based learning that current academic standards require. Such learning places the focus squarely on the curriculum materials. It is rooted in ongoing, active experiences that prompt teachers to change their instructional practices, expand their content knowledge, and challenge their beliefs. That stands in contrast to traditional teacher training, which typically relays a static mass of information that teachers selectively apply to existing practice.

Instead of a onetime workshop, facilitators guide a series of focused, small-group sessions that are structured like a typical day's lesson, allowing teachers to experience instruction as their students will. Working together, teachers rehearse lessons and address common concerns. They deepen their subject knowledge and fine-tune their instructional approaches, growing fluent in the curriculum's rigorous content and sequence of learning. Over time, both inside and outside their classrooms, teachers see firsthand how their day-to-day choices can increase or decrease opportunities for student agency and ownership of their learning. These experiences help reshape their beliefs and assumptions about what their students can achieve.

Effective curriculum-based professional learning requires the implementation of high-quality instructional materials. This vision of professional learning uses curriculum as both a lever and a guide, helping link teachers' actions and ideas to new standards in a concrete, focused way. Done right, it can close the gap between the experiences we provide for teachers and those we want them to provide for students. Given the challenges teachers and students are always facing, such learning is especially crucial to their success.

The Trouble With Teacher "Development"

Teachers, unions, schools, and districts all seem to agree on the importance of teacher learning. The United States spends an estimated $18 billion on professional development programs every year, and teachers spend more than a week's worth of time participating in them.[1] From training seminars to coaching and small-group study, professional development is a major investment of money and time.

But research shows that most of these efforts do not achieve substantial positive impacts on teacher performance or student outcomes.[2] Studies also reveal a broad gap between the short-term, isolated experiences that typify professional development and the ongoing, content-focused, job-embedded professional learning that can help teachers and their students excel.[3] Most professional development takes the form of a workshop that may not be relevant to every teacher who attends.[4] Even when learning is focused on a particular content area, it tends to be short-lived, with most teachers participating in no more than sixteen hours of activities—on the order of a seminar or two—in a year.[5]

Interestingly, teachers don't seem to have soured on the idea of professional development in general. They just want to get more out of it.[6] In a 2016 survey, 97 percent of teachers agreed that they "want effective, ongoing, relevant professional development," and 84 percent expressed a desire for "more professional development that is tailored to my needs." The topic they wished for most was "instructional strategies in my subject area(s)."[7] In a 2022 report about the professional learning marketplace, Rivet Education found that 96 percent of teachers thought the number-one factor leaders should consider when planning professional learning was whether it would help teachers effectively use their instructional materials.[8]

At the same time, most teachers are not yet using rigorous curricula aligned with current academic standards. Just 7 percent of the nation's elementary school reading teachers use at least one standards-aligned instructional tool in classroom instruction. In middle schools, where standards-aligned instructional materials are most prevalent, only about one in four English teachers and one in three math teachers use them.[9] In addition, most students still spend most of their time in direct instruction. In middle school science classes, for example, 92 percent of classes include lectures at least once a week. While 89 percent also include whole-class discussion, just 63 percent feature hands-on labs or other active learning activities at least once a week.[10]

Not surprisingly, teachers have been stepping into the breach and designing new types of lessons themselves. More than half of U.S. teachers craft curriculum for their students, either by borrowing from multiple sources or by creating their own materials. Nearly one in three say their principals encourage them to plan lessons from scratch.[11] More recent efforts report these findings are improving, particularly in states where the adoption of high-quality instructional materials is a priority.[12]

Is it realistic to expect 3.7 million people to craft their own curriculum? There is a long-standing myth that creative lesson planning is the mark of a great teacher. Studies have found that the assignments teachers create or find tend to be lower quality, not on grade level or aligned to standards.[13] A more consistent, equitable, and commonsense approach would be to relieve teachers of curriculum development responsibilities and let them focus their energy where it matters most for student outcomes—on classroom instruction.

Still, the impulse behind these efforts is correct. The curriculum teachers use matters greatly to student learning. Several studies comparing student performance based on the textbooks their teachers use have found major differences in achievement.[14] Using better instructional materials boosts student outcomes just as much as having a better teacher at the front of the room.[15]

What if students could have both? The positive effects for students are amplified when strong curriculum is paired with strong professional learning: not only are students working with more rigorous instructional materials, but they also have a more skillful teacher to guide them. One study found that when teachers participated in curriculum-based professional learning, their students' test scores improved by 9 percent of a standard deviation—about the same effect caused by replacing an average teacher with a top performer or reducing class size by 15 percent. When students' teachers used new curriculum but not did receive professional learning support, the impact was smaller, at 6 percent of a standard deviation.[16]

The implications are clear. Curriculum matters, but how teachers use curriculum matters even more. As schools and districts continue to make shifts in the instructional materials they use, and amid ongoing challenges, teachers deserve the highest-quality professional learning to support curriculum implementation.

Reflect on this:

1. How involved are teachers in your setting in the selection of new curricula and instructional materials?

2. What are the barriers (if any) to active teacher participation in such a selection process? Conversely, what are the potential benefits?

3. How might you implement the "mirror" principle—that is, that adult learning experiences should mirror the learning experiences of students?

The Challenge

We do not yet have a profession in which teachers and leaders consistently focus on student learning, regularly collaborate with colleagues and experts in professional learning cycles around improving student learning, and routinely recognize that using and adapting high-quality instructional materials is a mark of professionalism. In the era of college- and career-ready standards, teachers implementing the vision and promise of new standards, especially for students with the most needs, often lack effective professional learning grounded in high-quality instructional materials that help bridge standards into practice. Over the last several years we have had a system of high accountability and low support for teachers. Decades of carrot-and-stick accountability measures to "improve teaching" have done little to accelerate student learning and close opportunity gaps. Providing these critical instructional supports would help rebalance our system and concretize professional learning.

The root causes that have contributed to this situation include the following:

*   Instructional materials (curriculum) and professional learning are seen as two different issues.

*   The capacity of teachers and leaders to determine the quality of instructional materials is still developing, and opportunities for professional learning need to be considered.

*   As a profession, teaching often prioritizes the artistry of instruction as contrasted with the critical responsibility of selecting and implementing high-quality instructional materials to meet the learning needs of all students.

- Improvement strategies have tended to focus on the quality of individual lessons versus longer instructional sequences and units.

- Policies have focused on individual teacher quality and effectiveness rather than student learning, including providing the enabling conditions for learning, such as access to high-quality instructional materials.

- There are some critical mismatches between the research base of the college- and career-ready standards and the availability of high-quality instructional materials aligned with standards and the research on learning.

When states, school districts, and schools adopt new standards in education, it is essential to support teachers in developing the knowledge and skills involved in using new instructional materials designed to implement those standards. The influence of standards rests with teachers and the teaching practices that they employ in their classrooms. Ultimately, changes designed to improve education must be implemented by teachers. The burden rests on their shoulders. The classroom teacher is the essential link between the intended aims, policies, and programs and the students.

If we are to support the professional learning of teachers and improve learning outcomes for our students, we must invest in teacher leaders, professional learning designers and facilitators, coaches, curriculum supervisors, and school and system administrators. It is not enough for these leaders of professional learning to be good teachers themselves; they must also be prepared to work with adult learners and able to advocate, guide, and implement professional learning at the school and district levels. It is critical that districts develop the capacity of leaders for professional learning. In some cases, this may be accomplished with the help of external partners with both content expertise and knowledge about the change process, the research on how people learn, and how to design adult learning experiences that mirror the instructional and assessment approaches envisioned for classrooms with students.

Closing Thoughts

Leaders of professional learning have the responsibility to provide classroom teachers with opportunities for transformative learning, like the "strange transition" that Victoria Paredes experienced in her teaching. The priorities of more rigorous college- and career-ready standards require new ways of thinking about professional learning. These transformative learning experiences are grounded in the implementation of high-quality educative instructional materials aligned with state standards. The education community must successfully address these challenges if current reforms envisioned by new standards are to become a reality.

This book and associated resources are offered with one purpose in mind—to give educators the guidance needed to do the very best work possible with all students every day. Doing anything less will continue to shortchange our greatest resource and hope for the future.

Where do you go from here?

- What information was new and valuable to your efforts to strengthen teaching and learning outcomes?

- What do you know about the quality of instructional materials available to teachers and students?

- Is professional learning positioned to support teacher selection and use of higher-quality instructional materials?

- Does capacity exist to support the transformation of professional learning?

- What are some potential next steps to consider?

Curriculum-Based Professional Learning

A Shift in Practice

2

//

Where are you now?

- I am wondering how curriculum-based professional learning differs from other types of professional learning.

- I am curious about the shifts required to move toward curriculum-based professional learning.

- I am interested in learning more about the changing emphases involved in curriculum-based professional learning.

- I am committed to professional learning that helps improve teachers' practices and leads to better student outcomes.

From "Learning About" to "Figuring Out"

"I picked a banana, and I said a banana consists of carbs and proteins," the seventh grader begins, gearing up to answer two big questions about her chosen food—where does it come from, and where does it go next? She details the elements that make up the fruit: carbon, oxygen, hydrogen, nitrogen, and sulfur. Those include the ingredients for water, or H_2O, she tells the class—with an unwelcome addition.

"I remember when I went to Florida, and they had really stinky water, and they told me that their stinky water was because it contained sulfur." Ewwww. But her classmates notice something else about the ingredients list, too.

"You could have one substance and then take it apart and make other substances out of the same elements," another student says.

Then, the teacher chimes in. "So, we have this idea that we're building things, we're making substances—is it like LEGO bricks, and we're putting them together in different combinations?" she asks.

Bingo. That's one way the OpenSciEd curriculum develops students' understanding of scientific phenomena using a story line approach. The curriculum follows a logical sequence of learning and is driven by student inquiry. That includes the current putting-the-pieces-together exercise, which prompts students to determine what they know based on the evidence they've gathered so far and what they still need to find out to answer a scientific question.

In this case, however, the "class" is actually part of OpenSciEd's professional learning for teachers, and the "seventh graders" are actually middle school science teachers. Taking a student's perspective is a critical part of OpenSciEd's approach to curriculum-based professional learning. Both the curriculum materials for students and the professional learning experiences for teachers focus on science instruction that shifts from "learning about" to "figuring out" through phenomena-driven instruction.[1] Instead of students memorizing disconnected facts, they investigate phenomena from the natural and designed worlds as they build science ideas over time as a classroom community.

Each unit in the curriculum starts with a familiar object or experience, like an insulated thermos or a booming car stereo, and prompts students to explore the scientific phenomena behind it. After this anchoring experience, students discuss their questions, and a teacher helps them focus in on the science content and learning goals. (In the case of the banana discussion, the academic focus is metabolism involving food molecules.)

The curriculum is deliberately sequenced, based on an inquiry-driven approach, and designed for the Next Generation Science Standards. Whereas traditional science lessons often start with a teacher introducing vocabulary and information about a science topic, OpenSciEd's instructional approach prompts students to notice the world around them, ask questions, and seek explanations to understand the scientific phenomena at play. The curriculum is concrete and universally relevant, and it focuses on what students know and can figure out rather than what teachers know and can tell them. Teachers orchestrate discussion instead of relaying information, and students often ask questions their teachers may not be prepared to answer.

Reflect on this:

1. What are the changes needed to anchor professional learning in the use of high-quality curriculum materials?

2. What are the structures and designs that shift when professional learning is focused on curriculum implementation?

3. What are the benefits of making these shifts toward curriculum-based professional learning?

From Curriculum Developer to Learning Facilitator

Teaching involves a variety of challenges. Learning to prepare all students to achieve college- and career-ready standards can be pivotal in teacher development. Most teacher preparation programs focus on content and pedagogy divorced from the curriculum their future employers may expect them to implement. What if teachers were given the opportunity to learn how to teach by using high-quality instructional materials that contain exemplar lessons and instructional sequences? Many teachers today are expected to design their own curriculum using state standards with district scope and sequence documents and pacing guides. And when standards themselves change, the default for most educators is to realign current materials to new standards and expectations. As a result, teaching never changes, and students do not benefit from the intention of the adoption of new standards. Bottom line, how can teachers design learning experiences to address current or new standards using approaches they haven't experienced as learners themselves?

Instead of thinking of standards as a starting point for developing their own lessons, imagine if teachers work like learning engineers to understand the underlying structures and internal logic in high-quality curriculum materials. Rather than professional learning that focuses on content or teaching techniques in isolation, curriculum-based professional learning uses lessons directly from the curriculum to deepen teachers' content and pedagogical content knowledge. Teachers enhance their subject-matter expertise while practicing how to facilitate and teach complex content to their students (see Table 2.1).

When they are provided with materials, teachers sometimes perceive these materials as a "scripted curriculum" that does not honor their professional expertise and judgment. Developing fluency in a curriculum does not mean following it to the letter; instead, teachers develop a deeper understanding of how standards are translated into units and how units are broken into lessons. Teachers are still expected then to adjust lessons to connect to students' lived experiences, funds of knowledge, and individual needs and interests. High-quality instructional materials help teachers anticipate likely challenges, offer context and suggestions, and prompt teachers to rehearse instruction with a wide range of student questions, discoveries, and needs in mind.

TABLE 2.1 From Curriculum Developer to Learning Facilitator	
LESS EMPHASIS ON	MORE EMPHASIS ON
Teacher as curriculum developer	Teacher as learning facilitator using high-quality instructional materials to support student learning
Old curriculum realigned to new standards	Newly developed educative instructional materials that help teachers develop content knowledge and pedagogical content knowledge
Scripted curriculum	Educative curriculum that guides effective implementation and provides annotated support for meeting needs of individual learners
Professional learning that focuses on deepening teachers' content knowledge and asking them to apply it to their teaching	Professional learning grounded in using high-quality instructional materials that simultaneously deepen teacher knowledge of content and how to teach that content to students

From Disconnected Learning to Deep Dives Into High-Quality Curriculum

Curriculum-based professional learning provides teachers with opportunities to experience new instructional materials as learners and then go deeper into understanding the curriculum's design and instructional approach. Instead of a "show and tell" session about a curriculum, let teachers experience it. Teachers are active learners, like their students, who construct their knowledge and beliefs based on direct experience. Teachers need to experience curriculum and instruction and see how an approach benefits students rather than just hearing about it (see Table 2.2).

TABLE 2.2	From Disconnected Learning to Deep Dives Into High-Quality Curriculum	
LESS EMPHASIS ON	**MORE EMPHASIS ON**	
Curriculum orientation sessions that present information about new instructional materials to teachers	Professional learning sessions that provide opportunities to experience new instructional materials as "student" learners	
Professional development activities disconnected from the curriculum	Curriculum-anchored professional learning with intentional opportunities to reflect on beliefs about learning and teaching	
Training sessions that emphasize solely building teacher content knowledge	Facilitated conversations that address the connection between thinking and learning	

When professional learning shifts to experiencing the curriculum, teachers have opportunities to deepen their content knowledge by learning specific approaches to teaching their content that put students at the center of learning. Teachers also learn to translate new knowledge into practice by engaging in planning with high-quality instructional materials often with other teachers. Curriculum-based professional learning includes practicing teaching from the curriculum to help teachers try out new teaching strategies embedded in the materials and examine the results of how students respond. As teachers reflect on their beliefs about teaching and learning using well-designed curriculum materials, they examine experiences in the classroom, assess the impact on students from changes in instructional practice, and consider how the curriculum is helping support student thinking and learning.

Less Adapting and More Scaffolding

Education leaders, curriculum designers, coaches, and teachers promote equity by ensuring it informs decision making at all levels. Rigorous standards and expectations for what students can achieve must be at the forefront of curriculum selection processes, curriculum-based learning, and efforts to change classroom instruction. Underprepared students need support, but they also need appropriately challenging, well-designed opportunities to struggle and grow. To meet the needs of all students, teachers can use high-quality instructional materials to help shift to more equitable instruction.

Every student should have access to high-quality, demanding curriculum and opportunities to think critically. Every teacher should know how to scaffold learning experiences so that students are supported to engage with complex materials and activities. Equally important is knowing when to remove such scaffolds for students (see Table 2.3). Promoting equity means avoiding strategies that leave underprepared students out of standards-aligned learning based on their current skill level. If a discussion centers on a highly complex text, for example, a teacher can read the text to less-prepared students and engage their thinking at a complex level, even if the prerequisite skills are not yet fully established. When teachers develop deep expertise in both content and curriculum, they can apply relevant tools and supports to ensure all students meet challenging academic expectations.

TABLE 2.3 Less Adapting and More Scaffolding	
LESS EMPHASIS ON	MORE EMPHASIS ON
Lowering expectations and compromising the rigor of instructional materials for selected students	Raising expectations for all students by scaffolding instructional materials appropriately to ensure all students engage with rigorous content
Adapting instructional materials based on perception of students' abilities	Adapting instructional materials to meet the needs of students while maintaining the integrity of the materials

From Fragmentation to Coherence

Leadership is rooted in shared ideas and understanding, transcends individual titles or roles, and leads to a compelling vision for educator and student success. Through reflection, listening, study, and collaborative goal setting, teachers, coaches, and principals build an instructional vision that guides decision making and resource allocation and ensures a coherent and seamless learning experience for educators and students. Curriculum-based professional learning is prioritized over the many other opportunities that distract system attention.

Curriculum-based professional learning takes a considerable amount of time, money, and effort. For professional learning to occur, those essential resources must shift toward a shared vision of curriculum and instructional improvement. Leaders must be clear with themselves and their colleagues about the extent of the resources required and be ready to shift their thinking to make tough decisions about what to prioritize and what to put on the back burner.

Coherent curriculum-based professional learning helps teachers understand the structures underlying high-quality instructional materials. It guides teachers along a path to mastery, building their expertise through successive experiences and opportunities to reflect. By contrast, less coherent schools take a scattershot approach, solving problems as they occur. While professional learning can be responsive to teachers' evolving needs, its general trajectory should shift to a learning progression grounded in the curriculum (see Table 2.4).

TABLE 2.4 From Fragmentation to Coherence	
LESS EMPHASIS ON	**MORE EMPHASIS ON**
Instructional vision development reserved for select groups of individuals	Broad-based leadership representation in development and implementation of instructional vision
School systems attempting to implement multiple initiatives to improve curriculum, instruction, and assessment	School systems focusing instructional improvement efforts on curriculum implementation and curriculum-based professional learning
Curriculum procurement and professional learning services purchases being siloed from other district decisions	Curriculum and professional learning services purchase decisions being aligned to instructional vision and plans for achieving it

From Retrofitting to Establishing New Structures

Effective implementation of high-quality instructional materials must be a priority and drive decision making. Within a teacher's schedule, time to study, practice, and plan is essential to effective teaching, not merely nice to have. District, school, and teacher leaders can find time for professional learning in unexpected ways, such as by adjusting daily schedules, introducing late starts or early dismissals, or hiring floating substitutes. In some cases, the priority is shifting how already existing time is used. In all professional learning sessions, teachers must engage with their instructional materials in a purposeful way, driven by goals in collaboration with colleagues and guided by a well-prepared instructional coach or facilitator (see Table 2.5).

Professional learning is not one-size-fits-all. It should include a collection of research-based learning approaches that instructional leaders thoughtfully select based on the needs of individual teachers and professional learning communities at different stages of implementation. Summer institutes are the beginning, not the end. Curriculum-based professional learning requires work throughout the school year and takes different forms, including professional learning communities and instructional coaching.

Effective curriculum-based professional learning designs organize professional learning community groups by grade level and subject and establish curriculum implementation as the core agenda for teachers' time together reviewing student data, including work samples; planning and rehearsing lessons; or troubleshooting shared challenges. Curriculum-based professional learning must be ongoing and sustainable, which means it cannot be led solely by outside experts. Schools and districts must plan for the future by building in-house expertise and leadership pipelines.

TABLE 2.5 From Retrofitting to Establishing New Structures	
LESS EMPHASIS ON	**MORE EMPHASIS ON**
Collaborative groups organized by choice	Collaborative groups organized by grade levels and subjects using the same core curriculum
Using collaborative learning structures and professional learning communities to address several priorities	Protecting professional learning community time for implementing new instructional materials
All professional learning opportunities focusing attention on early use models	Professional learning opportunities being distributed across models that address early use, ongoing support, and capacity building
Curriculum-based professional learning limited to curriculum orientations and/or summer sessions	Curriculum-based professional learning that spans the entire year

Shifts in How Professional Learning Is Designed and Implemented

Teachers are often introduced to new curriculum materials in "training sessions." We even say that teachers have been "trained up" after participating in these workshops. Although *training* is often used to refer to professional learning sessions, those who use the term are rarely referring to the same thing. People can get trained on how to use a computer software application or a new device, such as a cell phone. But that does not mean they understand how it works or was designed. Rather than tell teachers about a curriculum, curriculum-based professional learning prioritizes letting them experience it. For example, experiencing new instructional approaches from a learner perspective can help teachers not only trust that student-led discussions can be productive but also anticipate questions and ideas that will likely surface.

Effective curriculum-based professional learning extends well beyond the launch. Veteran teachers continue to implement the learning designs introduced in orientation sessions and support each other in preparing to teach future units and lessons. As new teachers are hired, they too receive support to understand how to use the school's curriculum. Schools and districts benefit from investing in teacher leaders and other instructional leaders to provide immersive learning opportunities and ongoing coaching and other forms of support.

Curriculum-based professional learning designs offer powerful ways of changing teacher practice and beliefs. They include offering teachers evidence of what works and inviting observations, reflections, and discussion. A disruptive learning experience, such as putting on a student hat during a model lesson or seeing a lesson taught in an authentic setting, can launch a conversation on teachers' assumptions about instruction. Reflection should be part of teachers' cycle of learning and rooted in their experiences. Channeling teachers' discoveries and discomfort into new practices and beliefs is a critical aspect of curriculum-based professional learning. Teachers need ongoing, job-embedded opportunities to work with their colleagues, resolve cognitive dissonance, and discuss, update, and clarify their thinking.

Changes in implementation support are also needed. Effective feedback lays the groundwork for teachers to recognize their strengths and weaknesses and commit to ongoing improvement. Observations by peers and seeing others teach can provide a common, shared experience that builds a foundation for trust essential to risk-taking and change. Feedback that leads to growth takes many forms. One type comes from coaches and peers. This type of feedback is bite-sized and grounded in shared definitions and metrics of success. Another type is based in how students engage with instruction. Are they participating, learning the material, and remaining connected to their classmates and the process of learning?

And how we think about change needs attention. Change isn't the difference between before and after; rather, it's an ongoing disruption of thinking and doing. It requires adults to make and remake their knowledge, actions, and beliefs, which requires attention and energy over time. Important change happens over three to five years, not during a single launch period. Change is disruptive. It requires adults to let go of old ways of doing things and recasts their experience and expertise as less relevant or in need of an update. Supporting curricular change means guiding teachers to come to grips with uncertainty. Firsthand experience seeing that new curriculum materials benefit students can focus teachers on the benefits of the new rather than the loss of the old (Table 2.6).

TABLE 2.6   Shifts in How Professional Learning Is Designed and Implemented

LESS EMPHASIS ON	MORE EMPHASIS ON
One-size-fits-all approach to planning professional learning support for the use of new instructional materials	Different learning designs that support teachers at different stages of implementation using new instructional materials
Feedback and reflective practices used solely during the monitoring and assessment phases of the learning cycle	Feedback and reflective practices embedded in every phase of the teacher learning cycles
Change as an event that treats everyone involved the same	Change as a process that occurs over time and uses individualized support to accelerate implementation

Closing Thoughts

We have described fundamental shifts in the role of curriculum and how professional learning anchored in the use of high-quality curriculum is different from most teachers' experiences. We also described the shifts needed to create the necessary conditions at the system level for effective curriculum-based professional learning. We shared how OpenSciEd's approach to curriculum-based professional learning helps teachers see the benefits of experiencing the curriculum as learners. These experiences create more equitable instruction by helping teachers to effectively use high-quality instructional materials to differentiate learning for all students. And we identified how specific structures and ways of designing and implementing curriculum-based professional learning can shift to increase teachers' content knowledge, pedagogical content knowledge, and teaching practices using high-quality instructional materials.

Where do you go from here?

- What have you learned about the shifts toward curriculum-based professional learning?

- How is curriculum-based professional learning different from other types of professional learning? How is it similar?

- What do you think the critical components of curriculum-based professional learning are that could facilitate these shifts?

- What questions do you have about how to design and implement curriculum-based professional learning?

The Elements of Curriculum-Based Professional Learning

3

//

Where are you now?

- I am interested in learning how to strengthen the impact of professional learning to support curriculum implementation.

- I am curious about how the *Elements* provide a framework for supporting implementation of instructional materials.

- I am open to rethinking my entire approach to supporting teacher professional learning.

- I am committed to ensuring teachers and students benefit from investments in high-quality curriculum materials.

A Curriculum Challenge

When Charlotte-Mecklenburg Schools in North Carolina took a close look at reading instruction across the K–12 district, what it found was far from ideal. The district had adopted rigorous academic standards, but 76 percent of classes were still working below grade level. Instruction varied broadly from one classroom to the next, and achievement was suffering, particularly among students of color. Yet there seemed to be no shortage of energy or effort by district teachers, who reported spending seven to ten hours online every week searching for standards-aligned lessons and materials.

"There was just very little coherence across our district in terms of curriculum and equitable instructional practices," said Brian Kingsley, chief academic officer. "And that was not an indictment of our teachers. We just simply didn't provide for it."

The district gathered an inclusive group of educators, leaders, students, families, and members of the broader community to discuss what was needed in a new language arts curriculum—one that was aligned to current standards, included educative materials, and would be joyful and relevant to students. As a result of that discussion, the district selected EL Education's language arts curriculum, which combines sophisticated reading, writing, and discussion activities with civic-minded social-emotional learning and deep exploration of content themes. Instructional and school leaders committed to using the curriculum's educative materials, and Charlotte-Mecklenburg Schools contracted with EL Education to provide coaching and technical support for teachers. This was essential, as the new curriculum would affect not only what students learn and do but also the skills and understanding required of their teachers.

In Chapter 2, we described fundamental changes to both curriculum and professional learning if higher levels of learning and performance are to be achieved by educators and students. These changes are the foundation for the *Elements* of curriculum-based professional learning. While substantive in nature, they are well within reach for schools and districts. In fact, a growing group of public schools, charter schools, and districts are already seeing the benefits of an investment in curriculum-based professional learning.

Identifying the *Elements*

We decided to explore their work more closely, and that investigation led to early identification of a number of factors contributing to their success. We studied a diverse mix of schools and districts, all of which are successfully using new curricula in partnership with Carnegie Corporation of New York grantees. We convened a group of leading curriculum developers, organizations that support teacher learning, and their school and district partners, including Brian Kingsley from Charlotte-Mecklenburg, at the corporation's headquarters for a candid conversation in the fall of 2019. Over two days, and later in more than two dozen follow-up interviews with participants as well as their partners in the field, we asked questions, listened closely, and learned.

We wanted to know about the specific challenges they faced. What academic struggles propelled the move to a new curriculum and approach to professional learning? What logistical hurdles were the toughest to overcome? We also explored the actions that contributed to their success. What tactics helped reset expectations for what students and teachers could do? How did support from outsiders, such as curriculum designers, professional learning providers, and instructional coaches, help build a stable base for change? What learning experiences did teachers value most?

The students and communities these educators serve are remarkably diverse, spanning all fifty states and virtually every socioeconomic and ethnic group. Some are part of large, urban systems, while others are small, more rural schools.

We categorized what we learned from these organizations and then went to the research to see what it had to say. Across the practitioner settings and deep into the research, a common story emerged. From there we identified a core set of actions, approaches, and enabling conditions that effective schools and systems had put in place to reinforce and amplify the power of high-quality curriculum and skillful teaching. We call these the *Elements* of curriculum-based professional learning, or simply the *Elements*.

The *Elements* encompass actions big and small, from purposefully selecting a strong curriculum to planning efficient teacher meetings wholly focused on instruction. In the chapters that follow, we define the *Elements* and show how school and district leaders, curriculum developers, and organizations that support teacher development can apply them in their roles and communities. We also provide stories from the field that represent the *Elements* in action as well as reflections on lessons learned. Finally, we provide the research base that undergirds reasons for their success.

Taken together, the *Elements* offer a foundation for practitioners looking to undertake this work. They also serve as a call to action. This powerful approach to curriculum reform and professional learning knits together two influential aspects of a child's education: the skillfulness of teachers and the quality of the instructional materials they use. By reshaping current practices with the *Elements* as a guide, we can help teachers develop the skills, knowledge, and understanding they need to set all students up for success.

Reflect on this:

1. What were strengths and weaknesses associated with your previous experiences with curriculum selection, development, and/or implementation?

2. What factors would you identify as contributing to your successes?

3. What factors were missing and contributed to your challenges?

Introducing the *Elements* Framework

Building on the work of Corporation grantees and the research dive, we identified several features of curriculum-based professional learning that lead to improved practice by educators and better outcomes for students. This chapter offers an overview of the *Elements* framework and an introduction to the components it comprises.

The *Elements* framework includes thirteen design features and enabling conditions for curriculum-based professional learning. We chose to call them the *Elements*, organized them into categories, and created a diagram (Figure 3.1). It's a play on the periodic table used in science to describe the properties of chemical elements. All matter is made up of the elements in the periodic table. Combinations of elements form molecules and compounds that have different properties and chemical behaviors. Much in the same manner, the *Elements* of curriculum-based professional learning combine to form effective learning experiences for teachers as they learn to use instructional materials effectively. We organized the *Elements* of curriculum-based professional learning into categories that would interact with each other to transform teaching, again drawing from the metaphor of the periodic table. The first ten *Elements* address the purpose and substance of curriculum-based professional learning by focusing on design features. Design features guide curriculum specialists, professional learning leaders, and decision makers responsible for planning and executing curriculum-based professional learning that supports teachers as they use high-quality instructional materials. The final three *Elements*, referred to as the Essentials, address enabling conditions that define specific expectations of system leaders, principals, and teachers for implementing curriculum-based professional learning.

FIGURE 3.1 • The *Elements*

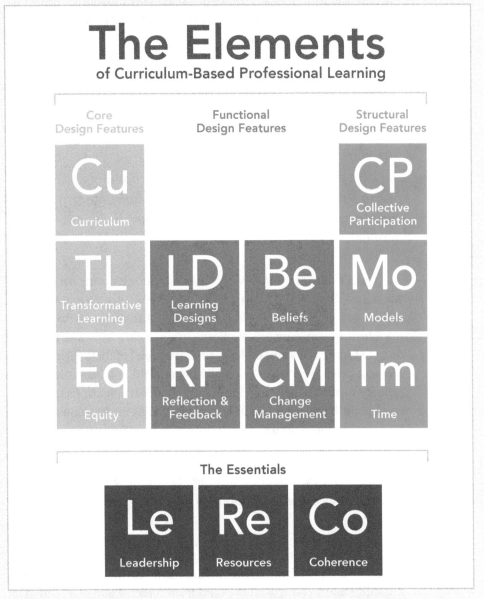

The *Elements* are the expectations and accordant actions that school and district leaders, curriculum developers, and teacher development organizations take to promote and design curriculum-based professional learning. They include:

- Core Design features, which focus on the purpose of curriculum-based professional learning
- Functional Design features, which shape teachers' experiences
- Structural Design features, which describe parameters and settings

Elements may be used in different combinations depending on what individuals and organizations need at different times. But all curriculum-based learning rests on the Essentials—expectations for system and school and leaders that nurture growth and change.

Core Design *Elements*

Effective curriculum-based professional learning transforms educators' beliefs, practices, and knowledge. Curriculum-based professional learning has three core Core Design Elements:

Curriculum builds teachers' disciplinary content knowledge, pedagogical knowledge, and pedagogical content knowledge by using high-quality educative instructional materials.

The first Core Design *Element* focuses educator learning on rigorous, standards-aligned curriculum that includes guidance on what to teach and how to use the instructional materials. Adopting and implementing a high-quality curriculum affects not only what students learn and do but also the skills and understanding required of their teachers. This *Element* privileges the instructional materials that teachers use as the primary focus for their ongoing professional learning. In fact, effective curriculum-based professional learning demands the implementation of high-quality curriculum materials.

Transformative learning changes teachers' deeply held beliefs, knowledge, and habits of practice through intentional design.

The next Core Design *Element* focuses on shifting teachers' beliefs, perceptions, and practices. New standards and curricula ask teachers to think differently about what to expect from students and how to interact differently. Rooting teachers' learning experiences in the curricula and providing opportunities to imagine or see how students may respond promotes the deep internalization and reflection essential to examining deeply held beliefs that lead to dramatic and durable change.

Equity articulates and advances high expectations for all students and applies culturally responsive teaching and content consistent with a shared vision for learning.

The final Core Design *Element* focuses the educator learning on the development of teachers' understanding of how to prioritize and promote equity through high expectations and culturally responsive teaching. High-quality curriculum is not scripted curriculum. It requires regular teacher study to consider ways to bring in students' interests, cultures, and identities. By walking through activities together before engaging in them with students, teachers prepare to support cognitive skills and habits of thinking that impart the lesson's key takeaways no matter what direction a discussion may take.

Structural Design *Elements*

Structural Design features include three *Elements* that describe the parameters and setting for curriculum-based professional learning:

"We're trying to shift the vision of what a middle school science classroom can look like. And those experiences and reflections with colleagues can really change what people are thinking and change what they think is possible— much more so than if teachers are sitting at home reading a curriculum the night before they go use it in their classroom."

—Katherine McNeill, Professor of Science Education, Boston College

Collective participation builds on collaboration among teachers in the same school, department, or grade using the same instructional materials.

Bringing teachers together in small, collaborative groups is a powerful way to support curriculum-based professional learning. When teachers focus on implementing high-quality instructional materials, their work is based on a shared vision and purpose. Through collective participation, teachers are grouped by grade or subject and have ongoing opportunities to study, practice, and reflect on using new instructional materials. Group sessions can mirror the activities teachers are planning for students, promoting empathy, trust, and a shared sense of responsibility and optimism for the future. Curriculum is at the center of the efforts, and collaboration amplifies its impact.

Models are structures for adult learning such as coaching, expert support, study groups, professional learning communities, institutes, workshops, and learning walks to achieve intended outcomes.

Curriculum-based professional learning respects teachers as individuals with different needs and levels of experience. It involves using different models for adult learning that support different stages of curriculum implementation, with learning experiences tailored to teachers based on their focus area, such as their grade or subject, and how long they have been working with the curriculum materials. Just as students need different types of lessons at different moments of study, teachers benefit from professional learning models that match their levels of knowledge and experience.

Time enables teachers to learn, practice, implement, and reflect on the use of new instructional materials during the summer and throughout the school year.

The wise use of time—with enough provided for curriculum-based professional learning for teachers at key moments—is necessary for successful curriculum implementation. Time goes hand in hand with models to enable an overall flexible approach that responds to learners' changing needs. The right amount of time will change from teacher to teacher and year to year, depending on individuals' needs and familiarity with their instructional materials.

Reflect on this:

1. Which of the Core and Structural Design *Elements* are most familiar to you?

2. Which of the Core and Structural Design *Elements* are new?

3. What questions are you formulating as you read further into the book?

Functional Design *Elements*

The Functional Design features include four *Elements* that inform the plan and implementation of curriculum-based professional learning:

"To substantially change curriculum and instruction, teachers would have to change their assumptions about their role in the classroom."

—*Sarah Johnson, Chief Executive Officer, Teaching Lab*

Learning designs engage teachers as learners through inquiry and sense-making while using the same instructional materials their students will use.

Learning Designs prioritize inquiry-based experiences for teachers and model the sense-making strategies teachers use with students. Curriculum-based professional learning prioritizes learning experiences for teachers that put them in the role of "student." Without these experiences, teachers are challenged to imagine both how their practice needs to change and the support their students may require. Immersion in student materials, video-based discussions, and classroom observations is key to supporting a new vision for classroom instruction.

Beliefs address teachers' ideas and assumptions about how to teach specific content, how students learn the same content, and how high-quality instructional materials provide productive ways to support student learning.

Functional Design *Elements* also focus on challenging teachers' beliefs to promote the Transformative Learning Core Design *Element*. Changing beliefs often begins with a disruptive experience, something that contradicts the tenets underlying teachers' daily practice or their assumptions about what they or their students can do. The goal is to promote cognitive dissonance—a state of discomfort that occurs when new information clashes with preexisting beliefs. This experience balances the discomfort teachers often feel in trying out new practices.

Reflection and feedback calls for facilitated time when teachers think about new instructional materials, receive input on how best to use them, examine student work and assessment data, and make changes to instructional practice in response.

The third Functional Design *Element* is Reflection and Feedback. Few people can learn in a vacuum—all but the most solitary creatures among us crave reflection and feedback on our work. Performance conversations contribute to each stage of the learning cycle for both students and adults. Without regular opportunities for teachers to reflect and receive feedback, their practice can plateau.

Change management addresses teachers' individual concerns and group challenges when implementing new instructional materials, including explicit opportunities to discuss and troubleshoot issues.

The final Functional Design *Element* is Change Management. Effective Change Management strategies ensure new curriculum and instructional approaches will last. Effective curriculum-based professional learning is grounded in a plan that supports both individual and organizational change. Learning experiences are designed and scheduled. Timelines are set and responsibilities clarified. And while careful attention is paid to detail, there is also a recognition that schools are complex organizations. At times, things may not go as smoothly as planned—which means that district leaders, principals, coaches, and professional learning designers and facilitators must draw from research-based tools and resources to support individuals and institutions to work through these challenges. Taken together, these Functional Design *Elements* link curriculum with changes in teachers' classroom practices to accelerate learning for all students.

The Essentials

The final component of the *Elements* framework are three necessary conditions at the system level for curriculum-based professional learning:

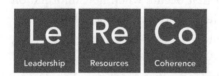

These enabling conditions, the **Essentials**, define expectations of district and charter school leaders and principals for supporting curriculum implementation by teachers and others. Each helps to build and sustain learning organizations, where ongoing investments in high-quality instructional materials and support for their implementation contribute to a powerful vision for instruction and success for all students.

Leadership commits district, school, and teacher leaders to a shared vision for learning and instruction that applies to both students and adults, creates a culture of respect, and supports necessary risk-taking for curriculum implementation.

In successful learning systems, teachers and schools work under strong leadership, with leaders who model and promote active learning for both students and adults. These leaders allocate adequate resources for curriculum implementation, including professional learning, making tough decisions about time, funding, assessments, and expert support. Such systems are characterized by coherence, with curriculum-based professional learning that both supports and is supported by other initiatives.

Leadership in a learning organization resembles teaching in an inquiry-based classroom. Like their students, teachers in such schools learn from their experiences, construct new understandings, and build on what they know about curriculum and instruction. Similarly, school and instructional leaders don't pretend to have all of the answers; instead, they ask questions, actively listen, and test out new ideas all the time. They model vulnerability and resilience, which promotes trust and encourages teachers to take risks, test assumptions, and break down old ways of thinking and doing.

Resources ensure that schools have adequate time and funding, high-quality standards-aligned instructional materials and assessments, access to experts, and the professional learning materials needed for sustainable implementation.

Curriculum-based professional learning takes commitment and resolve. District and charter school leaders who prioritize curriculum-based professional learning continually find the resources needed to support it. They have a clear vision of curriculum-based professional learning that informs their decisions about how to allocate time, money, and professional effort. When leaders make decisions with this vision and resources in mind, teachers are supported to study and use high-quality curriculum and instructional materials, participate in professional learning sessions with colleagues, and experience skillful coaching and facilitation.

Coherence aligns system and school policies, priorities, practices, and curriculum to a shared vision of learning and teaching.

Well-managed schools and systems operate on the same principle. There is no end to the running project list that energetic leaders or teachers have in their heads, and they run the constant risk of initiative overload. Successful schools operate with coherence, focusing efforts on a common purpose and selecting among competing priorities based on a central, driving mission. Their teachers collaborate as they strive toward excellence. They and their students work hard and maintain focus on what matters most. Coherence thrives in systems where leaders embrace a shared vision, one in which rigorous, high-quality instructional materials and professional learning are central.

Reflect on this:

1. Which of the Functional Design features and Essentials are most familiar to you?

2. Which of the Functional Design features and Essentials are new?

3. What questions are you formulating as you read further into the book?

The *Elements* and the *Standards for Professional Learning*

The *Elements* of curriculum-based professional learning tightly align with and reflect Learning Forward's recently revised *Standards for Professional Learning*.[1] Both guiding documents are informed by recent research and evidence about how professional learning results in sustained improvements in educator practices and students' learning experiences. Many partner organizations and education leaders participated in the conceptualization and development of both guiding documents, with many advisors participating in both discussions.

While the *Standards* address broader aspects of professional learning such as creating systemwide conditions for learning and laying a foundation for equity, the *Elements* are tightly focused on how high-quality instructional materials and curriculum-based professional learning can improve student achievement and increase students' access to learning opportunities.

Both guiding documents prioritize providing and faithfully implementing high-quality instructional materials and curriculum, recognizing that tying educators' learning to their day-to-day work in classrooms is essential to achieving improved results for each teacher and a key lever to students' equitable access to rigorous learning.

While the content of both guiding documents is aligned and complementary, their purposes, and in some cases their audiences, differ in scope. The *Standards for Professional Learning* guide educators at all levels in schools and districts to establish professional learning systems that encompass the structures, policies, and school and classroom practices to build capacity for every educator for any purpose. District- and school-level educators responsible for implementing high-quality instructional materials use the *Elements* to plan and design professional learning specifically focused on how those materials are used with integrity and can realize their full potential in classrooms.

It is Learning Forward and the authors' intent and hope that educators use these resources in concert—turning to the *Standards* to establish high-quality learning systems and practices and digging deep into the *Elements* as they facilitate professional learning with teachers around high-quality instructional materials to support curriculum implementation.

Closing Thoughts

This work begins with the selection of high-quality instructional materials. Charlotte-Mecklenburg Schools made this commitment when they adopted EL Education's language arts curriculum. The *Elements* offer a framework for schools and systems to guide curriculum implementation efforts and the focus of professional learning. They work in combination to support better instruction in all classrooms. Digging deeper into each will help you develop a better understanding and practical ideas for applying the *Elements* to your day-to-day work. Such effort ensures that investments in higher-quality instructional materials produce the learning environments and learning outcomes desired for all students.

During the COVID-19 pandemic, school systems that had previously invested in the selection of high-quality curriculum materials had a unique advantage when making the transition to remote learning.

Rather than spending time looking for materials for the virtual classroom, they focused instead on how to adapt already verified quality materials for the remote setting. The Center for Public Research and Leadership (CPRL) at Columbia University found that it was the combined efforts of educators, families, and students working with tech-enabled and standards-aligned instructional materials that contributed to improved learning experiences that better honored students' unique capabilities, needs, cultures, and communities.[2]

The CPRL study concluded with recommendations for sustaining a focus on what it defined as an expanded instructional core that included the role of families beyond the crisis of the COVID-19 pandemic. Districts were encouraged to add criteria that incorporated education for families, as well as tech-enabled and culturally responsive instructional materials. A greater emphasis on curriculum-based professional learning, particularly in ways that respond to student, family, and community needs and context, were encouraged. And finally, new systems and structures for designing, monitoring, and improving the learning experiences for students, teachers, and families could accelerate accomplishing goals for everyone. These recommendations and others surfacing during the pandemic years informed much of the thinking in this book.

Fundamental 4

Pandemic Learning Reveals the Value of High-Quality Instructional Materials to Educator-Family-Student Partnerships

1. Expand the required dimensions of "high-quality" instructional materials to include that they be educative for families, tech-enabled, and culturally responsive.

2. Leverage high-quality instructional materials (with the added criteria of educative for families, tech-enabled, and culturally responsive) to coordinate academic co-production among the four anchors of the expanded core.

3. Sustain curriculum-based professional learning focused on the expanded core, with explicit focus on implementing high-quality instructional materials in ways that respond to student, family, and community needs.

4. Create systems and structures for families, teachers, and students to design, monitor, and improve upon learning experiences.

Where do you go from here?

- How well does the framework align with your understanding of what is needed to support effective curriculum implementation?

- Which *Elements* were most and least familiar to you?

- Which *Elements* may require the most study and follow-up work?

- Where are you most interested in focusing first?

The Elements

of Curriculum-Based Professional Learning

Core Design Features	Functional Design Features	Structural Design Features

Cu — Curriculum

CP — Collective Participation

TL — Transformative Learning

LD — Learning Designs

Be — Beliefs

Mo — Models

Eq — Equity

RF — Reflection & Feedback

CM — Change Management

Tm — Time

The Essentials

Le — Leadership

Re — Resources

Co — Coherence

Core Design Features of Curriculum-Based Professional Learning

4

Where are you now?

- I am interested in learning more about what distinguishes the Core Design features.

- I am wondering how much of my current professional learning focuses on the Core Design *Elements*.

- I am open to rethinking my priorities for professional learning.

- I am committed to professional learning that will lead to the best outcomes for educators and students.

Charlotte-Mecklenburg Schools and Language Arts Curriculum

In Chapter 3, we learned that Charlotte-Mecklenburg Schools in North Carolina took a close look at reading instruction across the district and realized their curriculum needed to change. The decision to adopt EL Education's language arts curriculum was a welcome change for Principal Dianna Newman of Parkside Elementary School. A twenty-two-year district veteran, she had opened Parkside in 2015 with staff coming from ten different district schools. Teachers each had their own style, materials, and vision for instruction and student success, which often did not align with current academic standards.

"What seemed as though it was mastery for one person was not mastery for someone else," Newman said. "We were Googling for days just trying to figure out viable lessons that were aligned to the curriculum and aligned to our standards and our assessments. We really were shooting in the dark."

For example, Newman observed a fourth-grade reading lesson that was supposed to teach students to compare the main ideas of two texts. In practice, though, students were provided with short paragraphs and asked to name the main idea of each one, rather than reading complex passages side by side and identifying similarities in their main ideas. The fourth graders were actually doing second-grade work.

"The kids didn't have to write anything. They didn't have to share their thinking," Newman said. "There wasn't really an in-depth process that the teacher took the kids through, and they certainly didn't have to think very hard or very much to get to the correct response."

In EL Education's language arts curriculum, student work is organized into nine-week modules, each centered on a subject; in the early grades, these are kid-friendly topics, such as frogs or bird species. Daily lessons build students' content knowledge and literacy skills and include recurring writing, reading, and discussion activities. The teacher's role is to foster close reading, complex thinking, and deft expression in speaking and writing.

EL Education's professional learning is "built by design to mirror the pedagogical practices that are baked into the curriculum," said Amy Bailey, the organization's chief partnership officer. Instructional moves and strategies from the curriculum also lend structure to professional learning for teachers with features such as learning targets, "I can" statements, and opportunities for reflection. In learning sessions, teachers experience the same type of instruction they are expected to provide for their students.

"There are moments where you see a teacher is given a very complex text to read and analyze and think about and give a gist on, or follow a protocol, and they understand what it might feel like for a young student to be in a text that is really pushing them and is uncomfortable," said Bailey. "At our best, we are able to create an experience for a teacher that allows them to deeply empathize with the experience their kids are going to have. Instead of answering their questions, we'll say things like, 'Great question—keep working with your group.' It can be frustrating, but that's where we see real learning and engagement in productive struggle."

When Parkside's teachers met to study upcoming lessons, they soon began rehearsing components of each lesson. Participating in the lesson, either as teacher or as learner, was more valuable than simply discussing it; hands-on practice is a powerful way to learn. Having teachers authentically engage in reading a text and completing a writing task, like their students would, helped teachers anticipate how their students might respond. Teachers constantly make choices in the moment. They guide students' experiences. By walking through activities together before engaging in them with students, teachers were prepared to impart a lesson's key takeaways no matter what direction the discussion took.

After a few months, Parkside was filled with evidence of teachers' and students' efforts. Throughout the building, classrooms and hallways were decorated with writing projects. A third-grade teacher who had been uncomfortable with group work was successfully facilitating student-led discussions. And teachers were comparing essays with those from past years and seeing a major difference in students' sophistication of thought and self-expression.

"The shift was a difficult one for teachers," said Newman. "But once teachers realized that there is value—that these curriculum materials are beautifully written, and my leaders and my administrators are willing to work alongside me to help me get where I need to go—I feel like they embraced it a lot more."

Reflect on this:

1. How was the new literacy curriculum supporting teacher development at Parkside Elementary School?

2. Think about professional learning that you have led or in which you have participated. What are similarities and differences between these experiences and those that are described in the case?

3. What evidence indicated that Parkside's approach to curriculum-based professional learning was making a difference for teachers and students? In your experience, how have you evaluated the impact of your professional learning?

Curriculum-based professional learning has three *Elements* that we consider Core Design features: rigorous, standards-aligned curriculum with guidance for teachers on what to teach and how to use the instructional materials; transformative learning experiences that shift teachers' beliefs, perceptions, and practices; and the development of teachers' understanding of how to prioritize and promote equity through high expectations and culturally responsive teaching.

These Core Design features establish the purpose of curriculum-based professional learning. This work requires careful decisions by professional learning designers and facilitators, system leaders, and instructional coaches. Together, the Core Design features can elevate teaching and learning across schools and districts, ensuring every teacher is prepared to lead engaging, rigorous, and relevant instruction.

A Focus on Curriculum

"You have to understand the what and the why and the how behind each of the moves that are happening in the lessons."

—*Dianna Newman, Principal, Parkside Elementary School, Charlotte-Mecklenburg Schools*

Good teaching is rocket science. Teachers achieve this remarkable feat when they apply sophisticated instructional approaches that require a deep understanding of the subject matter and how students learn.[1] When they do, students learn and grow at a rapid pace. They take on challenging topics and complete in-depth assignments. They persist through uncertainty, grow more curious and confident in their abilities, and master complex skills and content.

Curriculum builds teachers' disciplinary content knowledge, pedagogical knowledge, and pedagogical content knowledge by using high-quality educative instructional materials.

Curriculum is at the heart of these efforts. A well-designed, high-quality curriculum charts a course for student learning by setting in motion a sequence of experiences that build knowledge and skills and create strong critical thinkers. Through textbooks, teachers' guides, classroom assessments, and other instructional tools, curriculum establishes the pace and pathways for student progress. Well-chosen high-quality curriculum materials can also do the same for teachers.

High-quality curriculum materials shape and enhance the relationships between teachers, students, and content. They establish what is to be taught, how it should be taught, and how teachers should engage with students to build their understanding.[2] These materials promote teaching strategies that support student discourse and help students make meaning from their experiences, as well as tactics for situating class activities within academic content and standards.

Curriculum literacy—the awareness of what rigorous, grade-level content looks like and the ability to implement it effectively in the classroom—seems to be an essential skill for every teacher.[3] In addition, curriculum literacy may include the ability of teachers to identify and remedy deficiencies in instructional materials they are given to teach.[4] Finally, teachers require curriculum literacy to translate their understanding of the subjects they will teach and the curriculum they will be provided in order to create meaningful learning opportunities for students.[5]

Focusing teachers' professional learning on curriculum literacy shapes how one becomes a good teacher. An increasing number of instructional materials are educative. Educative curricula provide teaching materials, student materials, and thoughtful guidance to teachers to strengthen content knowledge, teaching expertise, and specific disciplinary-based strategies for engaging students. Educative curriculum materials offer a learning sequence for teachers as well as students. Pairing strong curriculum with professional learning amplifies the power of curriculum to drive student learning.[6] It also builds teachers' understanding of how students learn rigorous subject matter best.[7]

Developing an educative curriculum is not an easy task. Curriculum developers have deep understanding of the academic content standards students are expected to master. They interpret learning sciences to select and describe the pedagogy appropriate for reaching the standards. They provide background; they set context; they offer explanations; and they suggest timing. They have the experience and insights that enable them to anticipate where teachers and students may struggle. They provide careful explanations of potential misunderstandings and ways to address and correct them. Successful curriculum developers have wisdom and insights from years of experience.

Another important aspect of educative curricula is how they incorporate an instructional model that supports how students learn and helps teachers shift their teaching practices in ways that are consistent with student-centered learning. One example is the BSCS 5E Instructional Model and its widespread use in educative science curriculum materials.[8] The "5Es" (engagement, exploration, explanation, elaboration, and evaluation) shift the roles of teachers and students in learning by prioritizing students' sense-making. Supporting coherence from the students' perspective is also the approach of the *storylines* instructional model where students see the work they do as addressing questions and problems they have identified, rather than following instructions from teachers and textbooks.[9] Storyline units are supported by a collection of instructional routines and norms that provide strategies and tools to guide teachers' work with students around content, questions, and sense-making.

Working with well-designed educative curriculum materials can transform the teaching experience.[10] Rather than seeking out supplementary materials or redesigning lessons that don't feel like a good fit, teachers develop a deep understanding of the underlying concepts and structures that knit the curriculum together. As they learn, they enhance their content knowledge and their understanding of the rationale for the curriculum's learning sequences. Instead of redesigning lessons, they spend their limited time preparing to use high-quality instructional materials nimbly, freeing up energy to foster relationships with students and help them to meet rigorous standards.

When professional learning focuses primarily on implementing these types of instructional materials, teachers have the necessary tools and support for great instruction and student engagement. Through ongoing and sustained professional learning, they develop the deep understanding and demonstrate the competencies that are the foundation of skillful implementation and ultimately adaptation of the curriculum to enable all students to achieve at high levels. District and school leaders and curriculum designers can promote student learning by ensuring that instructional materials and professional learning experiences help teachers bridge the gaps in their preparation. Curriculum-based professional learning enhances teachers' abilities to engage students with rigorous content. It expands their subject-matter knowledge and instructional expertise through study, practice, reflection, and feedback.

Teachers and students deserve the very best instructional materials available to guide their learning journey. While students will experience a variety of teaching personalities throughout their years in school, the quality of lessons and assignments should not differ by the creativity or expertise levels of the teachers they are assigned.

Reflect on this:

1. What is your reaction to the concept of curriculum literacy?

2. Think about the professional learning that you have led or in which you have participated. To what degree did it focus on instructional materials?

3. What changes can you envision if most professional learning was anchored in high-quality instructional materials?

Putting Curriculum to Work

This view of learning from curriculum and instructional materials (see Table 4.1) represents three major shifts from the way most professional development occurs:

- **From developer to facilitator:** Instead of thinking of standards as a starting point for developing their own lesson plans, teachers study and experience the underlying structures and internal logic in high-quality curriculum and instructional materials so that they can guide students through a well-designed sequence of learning.

- **Combine content and instructional expertise:** Rather than focusing on one aspect of a subject or on a particular instructional technique, curriculum-based professional learning uses lessons directly from the curriculum to deepen teachers' content knowledge. Teachers enhance their subject-matter expertise while practicing how to teach complex content to their students.

- **Talking points, but not a script:** Educative materials and support can help teachers become comfortable conducting learning activities that keep students on track to meet ambitious goals. They help teachers anticipate likely challenges, offer context and suggestions, and prompt teachers to rehearse instruction with a wide range of student questions and discoveries in mind. Obtaining fluency in a curriculum does not mean following it to the letter; teachers develop the deep understanding and skills essential to addressing students' identities, needs, and interests.

TABLE 4.1   CHANGING EMPHASES: Curriculum

Curriculum is a Core Design feature that encompasses the following changes in emphases:

LESS EMPHASIS ON	MORE EMPHASIS ON
Teacher as curriculum developer	Teacher as learning facilitator using high-quality instructional materials to support student learning
Focus on understanding grade-level and subject-matter standards	Understanding curriculum organization such as the instructional model and lesson structures or routines about how to teach the content
Professional learning that focuses on deepening teachers' content knowledge and asking them to apply it to their teaching	Professional learning grounded in using high-quality instructional materials that simultaneously deepens teacher content knowledge and how to teach that content to students

The Importance of Transformative Learning

"I think that for something to stick, and for our staff to be excited about it, they have to themselves see the benefits of it."

—*Dana Carter, Principal, Gladstone Elementary School*

When it comes to choosing what's best for their students, most teachers draw on their own experiences in the classroom. But those trusted techniques are often a poor match for today's standards and curriculum. Similarly, shifting student demographics may call for new perspectives and methodologies. Teachers are now asked to engage students with more challenging content and to cede center stage—to change both what they teach and how they teach it. To do that, they need to revisit their underlying beliefs about teaching and learning.

Transformative learning changes teachers' deeply held beliefs, knowledge, and habits of practice through intentional design.

Transformative learning occurs when professional learning challenges teachers' long-held ideas about what students can do.[11] For teachers to successfully use the new breed of high-quality curriculum materials, they cannot merely switch to a different textbook and go on teaching in the same way. They need to rethink their approach to engaging their students with rigorous content, and they need to reimagine what effective instruction looks like.

Tom Guskey presents a sequence of change that may seem counterintuitive to some (see Figure 4.1). Change in both teacher practice and student learning outcomes is required for change in beliefs.[12] This finding is often contradicted by the practice of education leaders who assume that shifts in beliefs and attitudes must precede change in teachers' practices. Too

FIGURE 4.1   A Model of Teacher Change

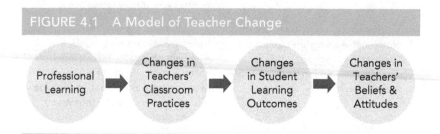

frequently, school systems hire motivational speakers to convince teachers to change beliefs overnight about practices or students.

Teachers are justifiably skeptical of inspirational promises from outsiders and experts. They are fiercely protective of their students and need direct experience with new instructional materials to trust that they can work. But teachers also are highly adaptable once the benefits to students are clear. Effective curriculum-based professional learning starts with experiences that promote changes in instructional practice that produce better outcomes for students. In many cases, these experiences are designed to contradict teachers' assumptions and disturb their equilibrium. One way to address the dissonance is to provide teachers direct opportunities to experience curriculum materials as learners, to discuss and reflect on the potential impact on students, and then to use these materials in classrooms with support and arrive at a new understanding of students' capabilities.

One way learning facilitators help teachers examine beliefs and assumptions is by teaching lessons from high-quality curriculum materials and asking teachers to engage as learners. Taking on a learner perspective gives teachers a novel vantage point, showing them what it feels like to experience the curriculum as a student and providing evidence that unfamiliar lessons can work well. A teacher could then teach the same lessons to students with support from an instructional coach, disproving the notion that the rigorous instructional approaches that sound great on paper won't work in a particular school or classroom. These activities build teachers' understanding and trust in the curriculum's design.

Transformative learning is a continual process. Ongoing professional learning is necessary to support teachers as they use the curriculum in their own classrooms and track its impact on their students, including giving teachers regular opportunities to think deeply about the structure and intent of their lessons. Through repeated cycles of learning, teachers try new instructional practices embedded in the instructional materials, reflect on and revise old habits, and change their practices and beliefs over time. This type of learning supports a broad vision for lasting change while still being rooted in teachers' direct experience.

Reflect on this:

1. Can you think of a time when your beliefs shifted after trying something new and experiencing success? What was that experience like?

2. Do you agree with Guskey's order of change? How does it reflect your own experiences working with teachers on changes in their classroom practices?

3. Why do you suppose this *Element* is referred to as transformative learning?

Putting Transformative Learning to Work

This view of transformative learning (see Table 4.2) represents three major shifts from the way most professional development occurs:

- **Experiences, not speeches:** School districts spend thousands of dollars on motivational speakers with generic messages of inspiration, and much professional development takes the form of onetime seminars or presentations. However, most adult learners construct their knowledge and beliefs based on direct experience. Teachers need to experience new curriculum and instructional strategies to see firsthand how an approach benefits students rather than just hearing about it.

- **Embrace discomfort:** Active learning experiences that challenge teachers' beliefs and assumptions enable new ideas and practices to take root. Learning experiences should highlight the disconnection between teachers' long-held ideas and students' ability to engage with new curriculum and instruction. For example, some teachers may believe that they could harm their students by presenting rigorous content and complex activities. Observing a classroom of similar students successfully engaging in debate, for example, may dislodge that assumption and build a foundation for new instructional practices and ideas.

- **Flip the script:** Assumptions are often unspoken and maintained by an unvarying point of view. Changing teachers' vantage points can challenge their beliefs and promote change. Taking on the student role in a lesson, for instance, provides teachers with hands-on experience and concrete insights into how they can engage their students in standards-aligned activities.

TABLE 4.2   CHANGING EMPHASES: Transformative Learning

Transformative learning is a Core Design feature that encompasses the following changes in emphases:

LESS EMPHASIS ON	MORE EMPHASIS ON
Discussing beliefs and assumptions	Engaging teachers in experiences that create cognitive dissonance and promote reflection on beliefs
Speakers selected for motivational purposes	Effective learning experiences grounded in high-quality instructional materials that include introspection of beliefs

LESS EMPHASIS ON	MORE EMPHASIS ON
Curriculum overview and planning sessions	Curriculum-based professional learning that asks teachers to take a student perspective when introduced to new materials

A Curriculum Lens on Equity

"Kids do what is asked of them. If you ask something that is low-level, they will do the low-level work and get As. If you give them something that is higher-level, they might struggle at first, but they will push through."

—HaMy Vu, Managing Director of Learning and Research, Teaching Lab

Ask any teacher to name the best part of their work, and the answer is nearly always the same: the students. Teachers are drawn to the classroom because they want to work with young people, and the relationships they develop with students are often the highlight of their career.

Those relationships form the foundation for equity, in which all students get the individualized support they need to meet high expectations for learning. But increasing standards and instructional rigor is not enough to address the current achievement gaps. Neither is it sufficient to instill grit or a new mindset. We need to develop independent learners by helping students evolve new cognitive skills and habits of thinking that will increase their brainpower so they can accelerate their own learning.[13] Zaretta Hammond calls this culturally responsive teaching, which she defines as

> an educator's ability to recognize students' cultural displays of learning and meaning making and respond positively and constructively with teaching moves that use cultural knowledge as a scaffold to connect what the student knows to new concepts and content in order to promote effective information processing. All the while, the educator understands the importance of being in a relationship and having a social-emotional connection to the student in order to create a safe space for learning.[14]

In equitable schools, each student in every classroom is taught a rigorous standards-aligned curriculum by a well-prepared teacher with high expectations for all students' success. And in equitable classrooms, teachers use rigorous lessons and culturally responsive teaching practices that honor individual students' contexts, backgrounds, identities, strengths, and needs. Prioritizing equity means ensuring that all students have access to rigorous curriculum and culturally responsive teaching from teachers using curricula that incorporate cognitive scaffolding, help build relationships, and develop social awareness.

Equity articulates and advances high expectations for all students and applies culturally responsive teaching and content consistent with a shared vision for learning.

Equity is more than an abstract value or ideal—it is essential to the lived experience of students in classrooms and schools nationwide. Too few students consistently experience great teaching, and too few teachers experience the professional learning that supports standards-aligned instruction. This disproportionately affects students of color, who are far less likely than their peers to have access to rigorous content and coursework.[15] Providing high-quality curriculum to all students is one important step toward equity. But the impact of curriculum may be muted if teachers don't update their instructional practices and beliefs. Curriculum-based professional learning can unlock the potential of new curriculum and ensure that all students gain full access to the same learning opportunities.

Every day, teachers tailor learning tasks based on their perception of what students are prepared to accomplish. When they teach students who are not yet at grade level, they often choose simpler, less demanding work that the students can complete independently, eliminating opportunities for them to engage with sophisticated content and complex cognitive tasks. During class, teachers may cut short moments of struggle and lead students to a correct answer to keep the discussion moving. Unfortunately, these decisions only enable dependent learners and not the cognitive skills and habits of thinking students need to develop into independent learners. Teachers may also mistake students' current preparation levels for their ability to learn rather than understand it as a reflection of their learning experiences to date. Yet research shows that when teachers hold students to high expectations, including those not yet performing at grade level, they rise to the challenge.[16]

High-quality curriculum can promote equity by creating a common foundation of rigorous expectations for all students. Instructional materials include strategies for teachers to engage underprepared students in complex, grade-level content and thinking. Lev Vygotsky described how all students have three levels of learning: things they can accomplish on their own, things they can accomplish with help from someone else (the *zone of proximal development*, or ZPD), and things they are unprepared to currently accomplish no matter the amount of help available.[17] Vygotsky's theory of cognitive development explains that students learn more when someone skilled in facilitating scaffolding helps them move from current to new levels of understanding in the disciplinary content as compared to tackling the content on their own.

Educative curricula can help teachers take an inquiry stance in their teaching by taking a facilitator role in learning rather than being the expert or "sage on the stage" in the classroom. Strong curriculum-based professional learning focuses on and models these facilitation moves in teaching and pushes teachers to revise their assumptions about what they and their students can achieve. In studying and using new instructional materials and techniques in their classrooms, teachers learn to foster the productive struggle all students need to gain skills and understanding.[18]

Zaretta Hammond expands on the notion of taking risks and learning in the ZPD and says it requires building trust and *rapport* to help dependent learners avoid the stress and anxiety that comes with feeling lost and unsupported in school.[19] The relationships that teachers prize are key to this effort. Students are more engaged when they feel their teachers care about them and believe they can succeed. Strong teacher–student relationships build students' motivation and confidence to take risks, work hard, and meet academic challenges.[20] They also give teachers the information they need to ensure lessons build on students' strengths and the knowledge they bring to class, allowing their curiosity, energy, and brilliance to come through.

Reflect on this:

1. How does the equity *Element* square and not square with your definition of equity?

2. Why do you suppose there may be some differences?

3. Can you imagine ways this approach to curriculum-based professional learning strengthens learning for students?

Putting Equity to Work

This view of equity (see Table 4.3) represents three major shifts from the way most professional development occurs:

- **Reset high expectations for all:** Leaders, curriculum designers, coaches, and teachers promote equity by ensuring it informs decision making at all levels. Universal rigorous standards and expectations for what students can achieve must be at the forefront of curriculum selection processes, curriculum-based learning, and efforts to change classroom instruction and underlying assumptions—especially when it comes to the daily decisions that can accelerate or hinder student development. In particular, underprepared students need support, but they also need appropriately challenging, well-designed opportunities to struggle and grow.

- **Scaffold, don't simplify:** Every student should have access to high-quality, demanding curriculum and opportunities to think critically. Every teacher should know how to scaffold learning experiences so that students are supported to engage with complex materials and habits of thinking. Promoting equity means avoiding strategies that leave underprepared students out of standards-aligned learning based on their current skill level. If a discussion centers on a highly complex text, for example, a teacher can read the text to less-prepared students and engage their thinking at a complex level, even if the prerequisite skills are not yet fully established. When teachers develop deep expertise in both content and curriculum, they can apply relevant tools and scaffolds to ensure underprepared students complete challenging work and know when to remove them.

- **Teacher–student relationships are key:** Students are more likely to be engaged, have a positive outlook, bring their whole selves to school, and bring a positive mindset to their schoolwork when their relationships with teachers are strong. Teachers foster these connections by showing interest and confidence in students' abilities and respect for their communities, families, and cultures. Knowledge gained through these relationships enables culturally responsive teaching and ensures that discussion and meaning-making affirm all students' identities.

TABLE 4.3   CHANGING EMPHASES: Equity

Equity is a Core Design feature that encompasses the following changes in emphases:

LESS EMPHASIS ON	MORE EMPHASIS ON
Workshops that focus solely on content or instructional strategies	Building teachers' disciplinary content knowledge along with pedagogical content knowledge and knowledge of how students learn using high-quality instructional materials
Lower expectations for some children	Raising expectations for all students regardless of race, ethnicity, and socioeconomic status
Compromising the rigor of instructional materials for selected students	Scaffolding instructional materials appropriately to ensure all students complete rigorous work and knowing when to remove those scaffolds

Gladstone Elementary School and Math Curriculum

To the untrained eye, Gladstone Elementary School in Kansas City, Missouri, seemed to be thriving. It was a nurturing, supportive environment where caring teachers taught energetic classes and students were busy and happy. But academic achievement in math was persistently below expectations. The school applied for a grant and hired Instruction Partners, a curriculum and instructional support provider, to study instruction and academic standards. They determined that lessons were inconsistent across classrooms but consistently below grade level. Math classes needed to change.

At first, teachers and leaders at the small K–5 school wanted to develop their own math curriculum. Staff believed they knew their students best and that with intense study of Missouri's learning standards and guidance from Instruction Partners, they could develop high-quality learning materials for their school. Teachers prided themselves on their strong relationships with students, and using an off-the-shelf curriculum seemed at odds with the customized learning experiences they wanted to create for their 440 students.

But that approach kept the focus on what teachers were doing rather than what students were learning. To substantially change curriculum and instruction, teachers would have to change their assumptions about their role in the classroom.

"They had really internalized teaching as something you do, and something you do to kids," said Valery Dragon, director of instructional support at Instruction Partners. "Although it was a great community, it wasn't necessarily a learning organization or a learning community. So, teachers as learners, I would say, was the biggest block because teachers were performers. And the fact that they were oriented toward performance never brought about instructionally relevant conversations as part of their normal experiences as teachers."

Gladstone's teachers and leaders, together with Instruction Partners, began studying high-quality curriculum alongside rigorous state math standards. Instruction Partners taught a sample lesson from the Eureka Math program, with teachers participating in the student role. This gave teachers direct experience and fresh insight into how inquiry-based instruction differed from their students' daily experiences. Then, as teachers gathered materials and worked to develop their own aligned curriculum over the next year, a fast-growing group chose to use Eureka Math lessons instead. All the while, coaches and leaders were conducting classroom walk-throughs to check whether instruction was in line with academic standards and offer real-time coaching and feedback. These classroom visits were informed by the standards-driven *Instructional Practice Guide* developed by Student Achievement Partners, which provides tools for coaches and administrators to support teacher learning.[21]

"Once the teachers started using the Eureka resources, the teachers were getting that feedback, and I think that gave them the encouragement— okay, I'm now giving my kids what they need, they're on grade level, it's scaffolded appropriately, it's sequential through the grade levels," said Gladstone principal Dana Carter. "And I think that excited them, just to be able to give the kids what we know is right, what we learned was right from our own experience."

Gladstone then moved to adopt Eureka Math across the school, with supports for teachers focused on learning the new curriculum rather than developing their own. Teachers rehearsed lessons in regular meetings for their grade level and recorded videos of their classes for coaching. During classroom visits, Instruction Partners coaches would model lessons, observe, and offer suggestions. Teachers worked to change common practices that, while well intended, compromised learning, such as not giving students enough time to struggle or allowing their own voice to fill silences and dominate discussion.

An ongoing challenge is moving from "watching" to "monitoring," Carter said. When teachers circulate throughout the classroom during student group work, they typically check for understanding and offer guidance. But more effective instruction also involves the teacher keeping track of common misconceptions and guiding students to identify and dismantle them.

Adopting Eureka Math was not a comfortable or easy process. But once teachers saw their students experience inquiry-based lessons, "there was an acceptance that what they had been giving students was not enough," said Dragon. And because the curriculum shift and professional learning were rooted in teachers' own experiences and built on a solid base of standards and research, they have allowed for the sort of "deep internalization" that supports dramatic, durable change, said Carter.

Otherwise, "I don't think it would have been successful at all," Carter said. "Typically, professional development in the district is basically an overview. 'These are some tools that you could use. Use this strategy.' But it's not actually going deep into each individual lesson. It's not preparing by playing the actual games that the students are required to play in the lesson, doing the actual math, having your questions written out. These are the things that we're working on."

Reflect on this:

1. How did all three Core Design *Elements* work together to support curriculum-based professional learning in Gladstone Elementary School?

2. Which specific changes in emphases were part of the story in Gladstone Elementary School?

3. How might you envision similar changes being enacted in your setting?

Closing Thoughts

Curriculum-based professional learning has three *Elements* at its core: rigorous, standards-aligned curriculum with guidance for teachers on what to teach and how to use the instructional materials; transformative learning experiences that shift teachers' beliefs, perceptions, and practices; and the development of teachers' understanding of how to prioritize and promote equity through high expectations and culturally responsive teaching. These Core Design features identify the purpose of curriculum-based professional learning. This work calls for careful planning and execution by professional learning designers and facilitators, system leaders, and instructional coaches. Together, the Core Design features can elevate teaching and learning across schools and districts.

We see in the two examples from the field how these three design features are core to the work of curriculum-based professional learning in schools and systems. Both Charlotte-Mecklenburg Schools and Gladstone Elementary School made curriculum a focus. After partnering with experts who helped them observe classrooms and review their respective English language arts and math curricula, they realized a variety of inconsistencies. Teachers did not have access to standards-aligned instructional materials, and as a result, students were not routinely engaged in rigorous thinking. Even though some teachers wanted to design their own curricula, school and system leaders did not think it would lead to a scalable coherent solution. After adopting high-quality instructional materials and supporting teachers with professional learning that allowed them to experience the curriculum as learners, teachers began to see students in their classrooms more often engage in productive struggle. Teachers learned to empathize with the experiences their students would have and transformed assumptions about their role in the classroom. They began to see the value of high-quality curricula and how it was helping them provide more equitable instruction to their students.

In March 2020, as the COVID-19 pandemic unfolded, we saw big disruptions in education systems. By May, most states either closed school buildings or recommended that schools be closed for the rest of the school year, with millions of public school students staying at home. Schools and systems were required to switch to remote learning, which required broader access to technology and learning new ways of teaching online. How to support educators, students, and their families throughout this transition became the priorities for school and system leaders.

But as living rooms and kitchen tables were transformed into classrooms, and the work of teaching and learning moved on-screen, it became clear during the pandemic that an additional set of actors would be critical for daily learning and instructional improvement—families. In September 2021, the Center for Public Research and Leadership at Columbia University reported findings from a study of nine school systems across seven states that included 294 interviews with families and educators during the 2020–2021 school year. The study revealed that the pandemic fundamentally transformed the instructional core to include families in the interactions among teachers, students, and the curriculum.

> As virtual and hybrid learning continued deep into the 2020–2021 academic year, and as families sat in on classes, coached students to sound out tricky words, and Zoomed with teachers to understand number bonds, their place in the instructional core solidified. As the instructional core expanded, the role of instructional materials transformed as well. These materials provided an essential coordinating and educative structure, assuring students consistent access to grade-level content, and guiding educators and families to deepen their understanding of learning standards, grow their capacity to support instruction, and ultimately, pool their collective knowledge of standards and students to make strategic instructional choices that worked best for their special context.[22]

Ongoing professional learning anchored in the high-quality core materials offered a focus for development and daily lesson planning; regular collaborative planning with coaches and peers offered new transformative learning opportunities; and a commitment to designing and executing lessons that met students' needs offered the appropriate level of rigor, honored their cultures, and demonstrated the potential power of a focus on the Core Design *Elements* of curriculum-based professional learning.

Where do you go from here?

- What more do you want to explore in relation to the Core Design *Elements*?

- What data might you gather to determine the degree to which your current practice aligns with these *Elements*?

- What benefits would you anticipate from investing deeper in these *Elements*?

- What are next actions you will pursue?

The Elements

of Curriculum-Based Professional Learning

Core Design Features	Functional Design Features	Structural Design Features

Cu
Curriculum

CP
Collective Participation

TL
Transformative Learning

LD
Learning Designs

Be
Beliefs

Mo
Models

Eq
Equity

RF
Reflection & Feedback

CM
Change Management

Tm
Time

The Essentials

Le
Leadership

Re
Resources

Co
Coherence

Structural Design Features of Curriculum-Based Professional Learning

5

Where are you now?

- I am interested in reading more about what distinguishes the Structural Design features from the Core Design features.

- I am wondering how much of my current professional learning addresses the Structural Design features.

- I am looking for ways to leverage the Structural Design features to increase the impact of my professional learning.

- I am committed to professional learning that benefits both educators and students.

Sunnyside Unified School District and Math Curriculum

Professional learning communities have played a major role at Sunnyside Unified School District in Tucson, Arizona, which has struggled with low student achievement in math. Nearly one in five students are English language learners. Some 80 percent come from low-income families, 85 percent are Hispanic, and 4 percent are Native American, as the district straddles First Nations lands.

Sunnyside adopted a problem-based math curriculum in recent years, starting in elementary schools and then expanding to middle and high schools. Illustrative Mathematics is built on student-led activities and relies on teachers to guide student discourse rather than lecture and lead instruction. Instead of focusing on direct instruction and coaching students to practice and get the right answer, Illustrative Mathematics promotes mathematical reasoning through activities and discussion prompts, including by presenting students with problems they may not know how to solve.

"There's tons of work around setting up structures for students to successfully collaborate, to know students and what they do and don't understand," said Max Ray-Riek, director of 6–12 professional development at Illustrative Mathematics. "To understand the tasks at a really deep level, so you know what the right conversations to be had are, and then being able to sequence and facilitate and connect a discussion that's based on students' ideas—it's really demanding."

Schedules for Sunnyside's math teachers included ninety minutes each month to meet in grade-band professional learning communities, but the district only had one math and science coordinator available to lead them. With grant support, Sunnyside enlisted Illustrative Mathematics to provide professional learning materials and instructional coaching with two goals: enhance teachers' understanding of the curriculum materials and build capacity to support ongoing professional learning.

During the 2019–2020 school year, various grade- and school-based professional learning communities met regularly in person and via videoconference to dig into the curriculum materials and identify opportunities to improve instruction. The meetings followed the same instructional routine as an Illustrative Mathematics lesson and focused on different components.

The impact of the facilitation and focus was clear. For example, when a sixth-grade cohort was discussing how to use the material's Check Your Readiness pre-unit assessment, teachers discovered a common problem: students were consistently forgetting how to apply the distributive property. They compared notes from classroom discussions and found that the confusion stemmed from variables, not the property itself. Teachers then made sure to share plain-language definitions of variables and give students opportunities to discuss and use them in class, getting to the root of the misconception.

These sorts of experiences helped focus teachers on the curriculum materials and transform their professional learning community meetings from general advice sessions to detailed discussions of materials and instruction. Often, meetings were used to determine which aspects of a lesson could be compressed or skipped without compromising student learning—critical to keeping unpredictable discussion-driven classes on track.

"Everything that's in our curriculum materials is so specific, and it's very necessary. And I didn't realize that in my first year," said Melody Salcido, a sixth-grade teacher at Mission Manor Elementary School. "During our professional learning communities, we've taken each piece apart. We looked at preassessment in depth, strategies for English language learners, strategies for students with special needs, the learning goals. When you look at everything so closely, it actually makes you realize how important all of those pieces are. That way, you can successfully implement a curriculum. I don't think I knew how to do that at first."

Reflect on this:

1. Review and discuss the last paragraph; what is your "takeaway" from the sixth-grade teacher's comment?

2. What *Elements* of effective curriculum-based professional learning do you see reflected in the Sunnyside example?

3. What supports might you need to engage in this form of curriculum-based professional learning in your setting?

Transforming teaching and learning takes more than well-intended commitments. As described earlier, the research on change involved in successful deployment of innovations provides valuable guidance for planning and executing curriculum-based professional learning.[1] We refer to the four phases of curriculum implementation as *laying the foundation, early use, ongoing implementation*, and *sustainability*. This book focuses primarily on the last three phases that follow the selection and adoption of new curricula or a decision to prioritize curriculum-focused professional learning in a school or system. There are practical considerations related to planning and executing the professional learning. For instance, how does the process of curriculum implementation intersect with teachers' daily work? What opportunities will teachers have to study the curriculum and practice new instructional strategies with colleagues teaching the same grade or subject? How much time is needed to support the transition to new materials, and how will it be allocated?

Structural Design features include three *Elements* that describe parameters and settings for curriculum-based professional learning across the phases of curriculum implementation: collective participation structures that enable teachers to work together to achieve common goals; models of effective professional learning to support different phases of curriculum implementation and others that evolve as teachers' needs change; and time, the most basic precondition for learning.

The Power of Collective Participation

"Teaching is often very isolated. Teachers have a room full of kids, but they don't often have a lot of time to be with their peers and colleagues to dig into teaching and push each other's thinking in complex ways. I think curriculum-based professional learning is effective not just because they have a curriculum, but because they have colleagues that they can talk with and push each other's ideas. The facilitator's role is to create a space where they can learn from each other."

—Max Ray-Riek, Director of 6–12 Professional Development, Illustrative Mathematics

Too often, teachers go it alone. Traditionally, they work separately from their colleagues, with limited opportunities for collaboration once the classroom door is closed. This isolates teachers from one another and prevents their students from benefiting from more than one adult's expertise. In recent years, unions and districts have worked to address this issue by adding shared planning periods into the school day, but it's not always clear what teachers are supposed to do with them.

Collective participation builds on collaboration among teachers in the same school, department, or grade using the same instructional materials.

Collective participation is the foundation of most professional learning models. Whether it be professional learning communities, study groups, or peer coaching, collective participation brings educators together who share a commitment and responsibility to advance success for all students they collectively serve. Collective participation is most effective when teachers are grouped by grade or subject and have ongoing opportunities to study, practice, and reflect on using the same instructional materials. This approach contrasts with typical professional learning communities in which teachers are randomly assigned and spend considerable time on administrative tasks or merely brainstorming and problem solving on issues of the day.

When collective participation is prioritized, teachers from the same grade or department plan, practice, and reflect on lessons together. In these professional learning communities, they examine data, including examples of student work; set goals; and compare their experiences using the new instructional materials in the classroom. Over time, they build a body of knowledge that enables them to drive improvement across a school or district. Research supports this approach, with many studies suggesting that teacher collaboration is essential to professional learning that influences classroom practice and improves student outcomes.[2]

When teachers focus on implementing high-quality instructional materials, their work is based on a shared vision and purpose. When they plan, rehearse, and reflect with their colleagues, they hear the diverse perspectives of others grappling with similar challenges. And when led by an expert instructional coach or experienced teacher leader, group sessions can mirror the activities teachers are planning for students, promoting empathy, trust, and a shared sense of responsibility and optimism for the future.[3] Teachers collaborate with their colleagues to build new knowledge and skills, working in much the same way students will.

Collaborative learning structures offer powerful solutions to the certain challenges of implementing new instructional materials. Within high-functioning teams, colleagues are valued sources of information, inspiration, and support. Previously untapped expertise within the group may surface when data are analyzed for what is working. Opportunities to group and regroup students to meet needs becomes a day-to-day possibility. Bringing outside content and pedagogical expertise benefits all teachers and the students they serve.

These cohorts become high-functioning teams with deep expertise in the instructional materials they use, with colleagues providing valuable information, inspiration, and support. They are essential to supporting ongoing implementation as well as sustaining efforts through the institutionalization phases of curriculum implementation. Curriculum is at the center of the efforts, and collaboration amplifies its impact during each phase.

The outcomes that result from collective participation and collective responsibility lead to collective efficacy, which promotes higher levels of success for both teachers and students. And collective responsibility is key to ensuring all students benefit similarly from investments in new high-quality instructional materials.

Reflect on this:

1. Are there benefits of collective participation that you had not previously considered?

2. How do your current or previous experiences with collaborative learning structures compare to the ones described?

3. What changes could you make to increase the impact of your professional learning communities?

Putting Collective Participation to Work

This view of collective participation (see Table 5.1) represents three major shifts from the way most professional development occurs:

- **More focus:** Save it for email—avoid agenda-driven planning periods or department meetings that focus on housekeeping. Establish curriculum study, practice, and reflection as the main subject of teacher and leader meetings, not an optional discussion item at the end.

- **More purposeful:** Assemble professional learning community groups by grade level and subject and establish curriculum study as the core agenda for their time together to review student data, including work samples; plan and rehearse lessons; or troubleshoot shared challenges.

- **More guidance:** Ensure that well-prepared facilitators are available for each professional learning community. Identify and support teacher leaders who can grow into these roles in future years.

TABLE 5.1 CHANGING EMPHASES: Collective Participation	
Collective participation is a Structural Design feature that encompasses the following changes in emphases:	
LESS EMPHASIS ON	**MORE EMPHASIS ON**
Viewing curriculum-based professional learning as an option	Accepting curriculum-based professional learning as a professional responsibility
Collaborative groups organized by choice	Collaborative groups organized by grade levels and subjects using the same core curriculum

LESS EMPHASIS ON	MORE EMPHASIS ON
Using collaborative learning structures and professional learning communities to address several priorities	Protecting professional learning community time for implementing new instructional materials
Limiting collaborative learning structures to professional learning communities	Using various collaborative learning structures throughout curriculum-based professional learning
Few structures to guide the use of professional learning community time	Well-prepared skillful facilitation and consistent use of instructional materials during professional learning community time

Mo
Models

Models That Support Curriculum Implementation

"The impact of the LEAP model can be traced to three major factors: high-quality instructional materials and curriculum-based professional learning, a broad commitment and the structures in place to commit time and energy to professional learning, and a culture of collaboration and social accountability for improvement."

—Chong-Hao Fu, Chief Executive Officer, Leading Educators

LEAP (LEarning together to Advance our Practice) is a successful model of curriculum-based professional learning that was developed by Leading Educators for the District of Columbia Public Schools and produced important outcomes for both teachers and students. Toward the end of this chapter, we will read more about it. While much professional development is often one-size-fits-all—think mandatory school-wide seminars or universally assigned courses—the format and content of curriculum-based professional learning is very different. It evolves over time according to the phases of curriculum implementation as well as the needs and goals of individuals and groups of teachers as they progress through them.

STRUCTURAL DESIGN FEATURES

STRUCTURAL DESIGN FEATURES

Models *are structures for adult learning such as coaching,*
expert support, study groups, professional learning
communities, institutes, workshops, and learning walks to
achieve intended outcomes.

Different assumptions about how adults learn, as well as the
desired outcomes of learning experiences, distinguish various models. Teachers experience multiple models of professional learning
throughout their career. Curriculum-based professional learning
applies specific models of learning that correspond to different phases
of curriculum implementation from early use to expert refinement.[4]
The models that are most germane to curriculum-based professional
learning include individual investigations, coaching, expert support,
professional learning communities, study groups, institutes, workshops, and classroom observations.

This approach to professional learning honors the curriculum implementation process and respects teachers as individuals with different needs and levels of experience. It involves learning experiences
tailored to teachers based on their focus area, such as their grade or
subject, and how long they have been working with the curriculum
materials. Just as students need different types of lessons at different
moments of study, teachers benefit from professional learning that
matches their levels of knowledge, years of teaching, and experience
with the curriculum (see Table 5.2).

TABLE 5.2 Models That Support Phases of Curriculum Implementation		
MODELS THAT SUPPORT EARLY USE	**MODELS THAT SUPPORT ONGOING IMPLEMENTATION**	**MODELS THAT SUPPORT SUSTAINABILITY**
Immersion in lessons as learners	Professional learning communities	Professional learning communities
Classroom observations	Examining student work	Study groups
Videos of classroom instruction	Classroom visits	Leadership development
Planning and rehearsals	Learning walks	Professional networks
	Reflective practice	Assessment data analysis
	Mentoring	
	Coaching	

Models That Support Early Use

The *early use phase*, sometimes referred to as the curriculum launch, leverages an immersion model typically employed in the summer and lasting several days. It is carefully arranged in a series of experiences, which will be detailed later in the discussion of the Learning Design *Element*, that prepare teachers to use early lessons and units with students. Rather than simply discussing the curriculum, teachers immerse themselves in lessons just as students would, participate in reflective conversations, and plan for the lessons' use in their classrooms. Classroom observations, videos of the instructional materials implemented in other schools, and insights from early adopters give teachers a sense of what to anticipate with their students. The immersion model could repeat throughout the year as teachers prepare for each new unit. When implementing a new curriculum, school systems often find it valuable to collaborate with outside technical assistance partners with expertise in both the curriculum and professional learning.

Models That Support Ongoing Implementation

Once teachers move beyond their first experiences learning to use new materials and into the day-to-day use of the curriculum, they enter the *ongoing implementation phase*. Models of professional learning often described as job-embedded are more valuable as they support teachers with the challenges and opportunities they face during daily use of the materials. Among these are facilitated professional learning communities that build curricular expertise and a collegial culture[5]; teachers examining student work and data together, visiting one another's classrooms in learning walks, and reflecting on their experience; and mentoring and coaching models that provide valuable feedback to strengthen instructional practice.[6] In robust curriculum-based professional learning, teachers are engaged in several models of learning that support where they are in the implementation process.

Models That Support Sustainability

The previous phases focus on the actions of teachers learning to use new curriculum. The sustainability phase focuses on the actions of leaders to ensure adequate capacity building and, more importantly, that the work sticks and continues. In the *sustainability phase*, leaders develop internal capacity to facilitate the work and rely less on external partners. They anticipate turnover and determine plans for taking new staff members through the early use and ongoing implementation phases.

STRUCTURAL DESIGN FEATURES

They develop talent pipelines for assuming coach, principal, professional learning, and teacher leader roles and responsibilities and establish networks of experienced educators to ensure professional learning and support continue for refining and adapting the curriculum for each group of students teachers encounter. Study and documentation of the impact of the investment in the new curricular materials inform the continuous improvement process and reinforce the long-term commitment to the system. Models such as professional learning communities and study groups shift teachers' attention from ongoing implementation to assessments and implications for refining and adapting instructional materials.

No single experience can achieve every target outcome in every phase. To put teachers in cohorts without first engaging them in an immersive learning experience, for example, would be to bypass important learning that informs the implementation of future units and lessons. Similarly, minimal benefits can be gained from taking a learning walk through a classroom before a teacher has developed an understanding of how lessons should proceed or worked with an expert coach to define an improvement goal.

Ultimately, each model fulfills a different purpose and requires different actions. Some work together better, and some only work in specific contexts. Some require more resources, including time, than others. To effectively choose and use models, it is important that leaders, designers, and facilitators know the key elements of each model, the outcomes the model is most appropriate to achieve (such as build knowledge, practice skills, or promote reflection), how the model may combine with other strategies, and issues related specifically to the model that impact successful implementation. Choosing wisely among models can accelerate teacher development and student success.

Reflect on this:

1. How does the description of the phases of curriculum implementation compare with your experiences with new curriculum adoption and implementation?

2. What are your experiences with some of the models we described to support curriculum implementation?

3. What opportunities and barriers do you anticipate in aligning your practice closer to the models *Element*?

Putting Models to Work

This approach to models (see Table 5.3) represents three major shifts from the way most professional development occurs:

- **A tailored approach:** Professional learning is not one-size-fits-all. It should include a collection of research-based learning approaches that instructional leaders thoughtfully select based on the needs of individual teachers and professional learning communities at different stages of implementation.

- **Consistent effort:** Summer institutes are the beginning, not the end. Curriculum-based professional learning continues throughout the school year and requires many formats, including professional learning communities and instructional coaching.

- **Looking forward:** Curriculum-based professional learning must be ongoing and sustainable, which means it cannot be led solely by outside experts. Schools and districts must plan for the future by building in-house expertise and leadership pipelines.

STRUCTURAL DESIGN FEATURES

TABLE 5.3   CHANGING EMPHASES: Models

Models are a Structural Design feature that encompasses the following changes in emphases:

LESS EMPHASIS ON	MORE EMPHASIS ON
Professional learning opportunities that focus attention only on early use models	Distribution of professional learning opportunities across models that address early use, ongoing support, and capacity building
Fragmented use of adult learning models	Integrated use of adult learning models
One-size-fits-all approach to planning curriculum-based professional learning	Explicit application of different models that support teachers at different stages of curriculum implementation
Curriculum-based professional learning limited to the summer months	Curriculum-based professional learning that spans the entire year
Sole reliance on outside experts leading professional learning	Building the capacity of teacher leaders to share responsibility for leading professional learning

Tm

Time

Prioritizing Time for Curriculum Implementation

"We are thinking differently about our professional development calendar so we can free up time and space, so we're not pulling people out of classrooms with students. There is a study[7] out there that says a sweet spot for our return on investment for professional learning is about 48–50 hours of job-embedded learning. So we carved out eight days of curriculum-based professional learning that is direct-to-teacher next year, and that's in addition to other vehicles, like communities of practice."

—Brian Kingsley, Chief Academic Officer, Charlotte-Mecklenburg Schools

Keeping pace with expectations for student learning is an ongoing challenge, and there are only so many hours and days in the school year. It's no wonder teachers routinely rank time at the top of the list of things that would improve their satisfaction and effectiveness on the job.[8]

Time enables teachers to learn, practice, implement, and reflect on the use of new instructional materials during the summer and throughout the school year.

Professional learning days and shared planning periods are already part of many teachers' schedules. But school calendars often are established by state regulations or employment contracts long before the school year begins. Such lockstep schedules give teachers a starting point for professional learning, but they are not sufficient.

The wise use of time—with enough provided for curriculum-based professional learning for teachers at key moments—is critical to successful use of new curriculum materials. Time goes hand in hand with models to enable an overall flexible approach that responds to learners' changing needs.

The right amount of time will change from teacher to teacher and year to year, depending on individuals' needs and familiarity with their instructional materials. When launching new instructional materials, teachers benefit from immersive experiences to build foundational knowledge and skills, such as a intensive summer institute. There, they can study the materials, experience lessons as students while being taught by a coach or teacher leader, and become fully immersed in the tools and approaches they'll need to start the year strong.

Throughout the school year, teachers ideally deepen their knowledge and refine their instruction by participating in one- or two-day learning sessions before each new unit. They have professional learning communities with others teaching the same grade or subject, with common planning time. Working together, teachers can develop a collective responsibility for their students and ensure that materials and instruction are aligned with students' interests, build on their strengths, and support growth where skills lag grade-level expectations. Professional learning communities can review and rehearse upcoming lessons, examine student work, monitor progress, and identify and troubleshoot challenges.

These professional learning experiences require more time on task than is customary for schools and districts. However, by investing time up front, teachers can develop a deep understanding of the organization and purpose of the instructional materials—and the mindset that the curriculum will be effective. And by setting aside time at key points each week throughout the school year, school leaders can help teachers stay the course and continue to learn and grow within the curriculum. Without these investments, schools are far less likely to realize the goals that inspired them to adopt the new instructional materials in the first place.

Creative district and school leaders can find pockets of time when they prioritize professional learning. Schools can occasionally open late or close early, giving teachers time to meet. Class schedules can shift to blocks, with student electives timed to release grade-level teachers during the same period. Floating substitute teachers and staff with leadership responsibilities can step in so that teacher leaders can participate in learning or observe a colleague.

These may sound like extreme changes, but such interventions need not last forever. Development needs shift each year, and even each month. Ongoing learning requires flexibility, not a particular way of allocating or spending teachers' time.

We can look to high-performing systems around the world to see the importance of devoting time to teacher learning. In some other countries, teachers spend 20 to 40 percent of each workday working with colleagues and individually to advance school and team goals.[9] Peer networks are predominantly used to support the implementation of instructional programs, including new curriculum materials. Learning time for educators often extends into after-school sessions, summer learning experiences, and times during the workday when students are not present.

STRUCTURAL DESIGN FEATURES

The COVID-19 pandemic raised issues related to the structure of the school year and school day. More educators expressed the need for time for collaborative planning and problem solving. Parents and caregivers expressed frustration with the traditional school calendar and school day, particularly recognizing the number of days their children missed since March 2020. Their shared interests and concerns prompted think tanks and professional associations to take another look at the issue. Some of these reports focused on restructuring schools to support the needs of families.

> *COVID-19 is laying bare two realities in education: Schools are not making the most of the time they have with students, and the school calendar is not friendly to working families. We have been warned about these issues for several decades, but the pandemic has brought them to the forefront in a way that we would not have seen in an otherwise regular school year. This is the moment to imagine and move toward a new vision of school that rethinks how schools use time.[10]*

A word of caution. Accompany any investment in time with an equal investment in how the time is actually used. Teachers can say they want more time for professional learning, yet there are potentially many distractions that may keep them from it. Merely providing the time without the support and guidance for effective use can undermine the entire curriculum implementation investment. Research on learning models and learning designs provides guidance for structuring time.

Reflect on this:

1. How is time currently allocated for professional learning in your school or system?

2. How much time is allocated to support curriculum-based professional learning currently?

3. Can you imagine where additional time might be found?

Putting Time to Work

This approach to time use (see Table 5.4) represents three major shifts from the way most professional development occurs:

- **Make a commitment:** Effective implementation of high-quality instructional materials must be a priority and drive decision making. Within a teacher's schedule, time to study, practice, and plan is critical to effective teaching, not merely nice to have.

- **Get creative:** District, school, and teacher leaders can find time for professional learning in unexpected ways, such as by adjusting daily schedules, introducing late starts or early dismissals, or hiring floating substitutes.

- **Be intentional:** It's not about time itself but about how that time is used. In all professional learning sessions, teachers must engage with their instructional materials in a purposeful way, driven by goals in collaboration with colleagues and guided by a well-prepared instructional coach or facilitator.

STRUCTURAL DESIGN FEATURES

TABLE 5.4 CHANGING EMPHASES: Time

Time is a Structural Design feature that encompasses the following changes in emphases:

LESS EMPHASIS ON	MORE EMPHASIS ON
One-day orientation on new instructional materials	Intensive summer institutes that immerse teachers as learners in new instructional materials
Monthly two-hour professional learning community meetings where the focus varies	Bimonthly three- to four-hour professional learning community meetings focused on implementing instructional materials
Contract-driven schedule setting	Teacher-driven schedule setting
Inflexible definitions of school year calendar and school day schedules	Flexible interpretations of school year calendar and school day schedules
Limited compensation and support for additional time invested in curriculum implementation	Recognition and compensation for additional time required for curriculum implementation

District of Columbia Public Schools and Math Curriculum

Every week, teachers met with their colleagues for in-depth curriculum study, practice, and planning at the District of Columbia Public Schools (DCPS). Each team was carefully composed by subject and grade band.

Facilitated by a well-prepared instructional leader, teachers reviewed student data and progress, rehearsed lessons, and reflected on recent classes as they planned.

These sessions were part of the LEAP program, which the DCPS launched with Leading Educators in 2016. LEAP was used in all 116 of the district's public schools, where student proficiency on annual tests increased by 15 percent in reading and 11.5 percent in math in four years.

"Prior to LEAP, in my experience, teachers who received in-house coaching were teachers who were struggling. And there was this idea that teachers who were really strong or who were really doing well in the classroom didn't need the support," said Libby Sanchez, a teacher leader at Marie Reed Elementary School. "So, one thing I appreciate now is . . . there's this recognition that all teachers deserve an opportunity to grow, and they need and deserve an opportunity to get better in their practice."

LEAP's laser focus on high-quality instructional materials, such as those from the Eureka Math curriculum the district adopted, set it apart from other teacher development efforts. It was school-based and specific to the content that teachers and their students were grappling with at a particular moment. Teaching teams followed a sequence of adult learning content that lined up with the classroom curriculum.

Over a three-week cycle, teachers and coaches met in professional learning communities, where they reviewed lessons in detail and selected a relevant instructional skill to focus on. Teachers then planned a lesson from the curriculum materials that drew on that skill and practiced it with their students. They reflected with their colleagues and experienced frequent observations—more than thirty each school year—to get the feedback they needed to refine and improve their instruction. Ongoing conversations stressed the importance of building students' academic skills and sophistication for success.

The program's keystone was its six hundred LEAP leaders, who served as instructional leaders and coaches at their schools as part of the district's Teacher Leadership Initiative.[11] About six hundred teacher leaders participated in a two-week summer institute at the program's launch. For seven days each school year, they attended district-wide professional learning sessions to analyze implementation data, refine their instructional leadership and coaching skills, and address challenges. These teacher leaders guided well-planned learning activities that shifted throughout the year, responding to different needs and building different capacities as teachers learned and grew.

According to Chong-Hao Fu, chief executive officer at Leading Educators, "The impact of this model can be traced to three major factors: high-quality instructional materials and curriculum-based professional learning, a broad commitment and the structures in place to commit time and energy to professional learning, and a culture of collaboration and social accountability for improvement.

"We know that quality matters dramatically in terms of whether teacher learning will yield positive cultural benefits as well as increased student learning," he said. "DCPS adopted high-quality instructional materials, and almost all of the work was curriculum-specific, which meant that teacher learning was anchored in what student learning would be. And that also gave the opportunity for teachers to understand the design principles and learning science behind a strong curriculum."

Reflect on this:

1. How did all three Structural Design *Elements* work together to support curriculum-based professional learning in the LEAP program?

2. In the LEAP program, which *Elements* contributed substantively to teacher learning and student learning?

3. What are the key takeaways for your work from the DCPS curriculum implementation efforts?

Closing Thoughts

Curriculum-based professional learning has three Structural Design *Elements*: collective participation structures that enable teachers to work together to achieve common goals; models of effective professional learning that evolve as teachers' needs change; and time, the most basic precondition for learning. These Structural Design features provide guidance on the setting and parameters for effective curriculum-based professional learning. Much of this work is overseen by professional learning designers and facilitators, system leaders, and instructional coaches.

In the two examples from the field, all three Structural Design *Elements* were present. Both Sunnyside and DCPS partnered with a professional learning organization to support the early use phase. These organizations designed and implemented the immersive learning experience model that contributed to teacher acceptance and confidence during their early use of the curriculum. In both cases, this phase lasted for a full school year. They leveraged professional learning community models for support of ongoing implementation. They purposely identified and built teacher and coach capacity to support ongoing implementation and in anticipation of reaching the sustainability phase. As you read in both stories, new time was identified to support the launch as well as provide ongoing in-class support. DCPS teachers were compensated for participation in summer institutes, and Sunnyside brought in extra help to provide the classroom-based support teachers requested. Collective participation was central to all learning models and designs. Professional learning communities were restructured to ensure members were working with the same instructional materials at the same grade level. Support among teachers during and outside professional learning communities demonstrated the collective responsibility for the success of all students rather than only those assigned to the individual teachers. And both school systems documented the impact of their efforts. Together, with the Core and Functional Design features that you will read about in Chapter 6, they elevated teaching and learning for educators and their students.

Jennifer Bland is an education policy researcher at the Learning Policy Institute who wrote about the impact of the pandemic on educators. She reported on the impact of a shift to more intentional collaboration to support coherent implementation of the math curriculum in Petaluma Unified School District in California:

> *This focus on collaboration was a substantial change from a culture in which teachers were seen as consistently dedicated but highly individualized in their instruction. More broadly, . . . the pandemic "pushed people out of their comfort zone and routine and made them question a lot of things that we took for granted." Those questions, including increased curiosity among teachers about how they might change their own practices, created the conditions for a new approach to teacher collaboration, among other changes. Petaluma administrators expect these innovations and cultural shifts to endure, due to their reception among teachers, and plan to continue providing the structure and support to extend and deepen this work.*[12]

What is especially compelling about Petaluma's experience is that the work did not stop once elementary teachers got on the same page about the sequencing of math curriculum. Instead, teachers extended their efforts to make other high-quality, research-validated shifts in how they collaborate around math instruction. The need for collaborative learning structures, effective professional learning models, and time has always been the foundation for effective adult learning that leads to better student outcomes.[13] The pandemic affirmed their importance as well as giving us new ways to approach them, particularly when planning for curriculum-based professional learning.

Where do you go from here?

- What more do you want to learn to put the Structural Design *Elements* into action?

- How do the Structural Design *Elements* contribute to successful professional learning?

- What are critical connections among the Structural Design *Elements*?

- What next actions will you pursue?

The Elements

of Curriculum-Based Professional Learning

Core
Design Features

Functional
Design Features

Structural
Design Features

Cu
Curriculum

CP
Collective
Participation

TL
Transformative
Learning

LD
Learning
Designs

Be
Beliefs

Mo
Models

Eq
Equity

RF
Reflection &
Feedback

CM
Change
Management

Tm
Time

The Essentials

Le
Leadership

Re
Resources

Co
Coherence

Functional Design Features of Curriculum-Based Professional Learning

6

//

Where are you now?

- I am interested in reading more about Functional Design features in curriculum-based professional learning.

- I am wondering how the Functional Design features work together.

- I am open to rethinking how professional learning works when focused on curriculum implementation.

- I am committed to professional learning designs that provide teachers with opportunities to be "learners" experiencing the materials they will use in the classroom.

Boston Public Schools and Science Curriculum

"It's a shift you have to make, to become comfortable with not knowing the answers and that being okay, and really relying heavily on student input. They are the ones driving the car," said Roselynn Rodriguez, who piloted the OpenSciEd middle school science curriculum with her students at the Rafael Hernández Dual Language K–8 School in Boston. "That can seem a little scary at first, but it's actually something that I really appreciated from participating in the professional development that we were provided, practicing that."

The Boston pilot began with a four-day professional learning foundational program over the summer for two dozen district teachers—an "anchoring experience" of sorts. Teachers in Grades 6, 7, and 8 began by watching and discussing videos of lessons that demonstrated the instructional routines in the OpenSciEd instructional model. Afterward, they met in small groups to learn how these routines are used in specific units. They then put on a learner hat and experienced lessons from those units as their students would.

"It's been an effective approach for the district. We prepared to adopt OpenSciEd more broadly," said Marianne Dunne, senior project coordinator with the Boston Public Schools Science Department.

"They do a lot of shifting perspective," said Dunne. "What will your students be doing and saying? What might they come up with? That's a feature for me that I think is really powerful. Because teachers will be like, 'Wait, what if it doesn't go this way? How am I going to know what to do?' And then we put our teacher hats back on and discuss: here's what we've seen, and here's how it goes."

OpenSciEd professional learning continued throughout the school year. During the winter, teachers gathered again for a two-day workshop before starting a new unit. They practiced lessons and explored topics they chose through a survey, such as formative and summative assessments and differentiation using principles of Universal Design for Learning (UDL).

Survey data revealed critical changes in teachers' beliefs about science teaching. By experiencing the curriculum as students, teachers temporarily discarded their scientific knowledge and encountered the questions as their students would. This prevented them from skipping ahead and helped them distinguish between wrong answers and incomplete learning. An important mental shift took place as teachers came to trust students at all levels of academic performance to engage with complex, rigorous thinking and content.

"One of the areas in which we saw a real shift in beliefs is whether or not you need to preteach vocabulary and science ideas to kids. Do I need to start off my thermal energy unit by defining thermal energy, and then the rest of the unit is just reinforcing that? OpenSciEd has really flipped that— you're starting with the kids' language and with the kids' ideas, which can help support much greater equity in terms of engaging a much wider range of students who are bringing different backgrounds and resources to the classroom," said Katherine McNeill, a professor of science education at Boston College, who led the development of OpenSciEd's professional learning curriculum.

"We're trying to shift the vision of what a middle school science classroom can look like," McNeill said. "And those experiences and reflections with colleagues can really change what people are thinking and change what they think is possible—much more so than if teachers are sitting at home reading a curriculum the night before they go use it in their classroom."

Reflect on this:

1. How does OpenSciEd's approach to curriculum-based professional learning compare to your experiences learning to use new instructional materials?

2. What could teachers learn by putting on a student hat and experiencing lessons as learners?

3. How might this form of professional learning help shift your beliefs about teaching science?

Effectively designed curriculum-based professional learning for teachers incorporates the same lessons found in the instructional materials used with students. It is rooted in sequenced learning experiences that focus on teachers' underlying beliefs, progressively deepen their understanding, and promote enduring changes in their practices.

In this chapter, we explore the four *Elements* of Functional Design that inform how curriculum-based professional learning works when designed and implemented. Learning designs prioritize inquiry-based experiences for teachers and model the sense-making strategies teachers will use with students. They also challenge teachers' beliefs and promote transformative learning, offer opportunities to deepen understanding through reflection and feedback, and include effective change management strategies that ensure new curriculum and instructional approaches will last. Taken together, these *Elements* link curriculum with changes in teachers' classroom practices to accelerate learning for all students.

FUNCTIONAL DESIGN FEATURES

 Learning Designs That Transform Teachers

"It at times can feel slightly corny to pretend you're a seventh grader, but I think it's really necessary so you're comfortable with the awkward silences that could happen in your classroom. . . . That thinking time, trusting what your students are saying and asking, trusting that it comes together—that was the biggest shift for me."

—Roselynn Rodriguez, Middle School Science Teacher, Boston Public Schools

Powerful learning is the result of deliberate design. Strong curriculum-based professional learning is inspired by a new vision for teaching that is guided by subject matter and specific instructional materials. These experiences are shaped by learning designs that build on teachers' empathy for their students and challenge their beliefs about what students can do.

All professional learning is planned based on what designs for learning will lead to the outcomes sought for educators and students. This includes setting relevant and contextualized learning goals, applying the science of learning, and implementing evidence-based learning designs.[1] Curriculum-based professional learning prioritizes learning designs that are anchored in the use of high-quality instructional materials and allow teachers to experience the instruction their students will receive. These designs will vary depending on the disciplinary content of the curriculum. How one teaches English language arts, math, or science differs in part because the discipline is different. Although these content differences may lead at times to different learning designs, the goals are consistent with a focus on inquiry and sense-making as teachers learn to use high-quality curricula. Well-designed educative curricula incorporate the science of learning through the instructional models and routines used in the materials. Learning designs incorporate these routines into professional learning through immersive activities anchored in the curriculum. And evidence suggests that professional learning is most effective when teachers are collectively engaged in subject-matter content with examples of effective instruction and the analysis of student work.[2] Working with high-quality instructional materials offers ample opportunities to deepen content knowledge and learn together about instruction and student thinking.

Learning designs engage teachers as learners through inquiry and sense-making while using the same instructional materials their students will use.

In science, for example, this vision for instruction involves teachers prompting students to observe and ask questions to investigate the world around them and build a complex understanding on that foundation. Rather than introducing scientific concepts and language in the abstract, teachers have students reflect on concrete experiences and use evidence to develop models and construct explanations. Students don't primarily learn by reading about science; rather, they reason their way to scientific knowledge as they develop models that explain everyday phenomena.

Effective curriculum-based professional learning operates in a similar manner. Curriculum-based professional learning experiences are most successful when they are designed to move teachers through different phases of curriculum implementation using both learner and teacher lenses.[3] Like their students, teachers engage in sense-making, though that plays out differently because teachers have different needs and more experiences.

When teachers are laying the foundation or in the early use phase of curriculum implementation and first encounter new instructional materials, professional learning begins with an in-depth look at how they are organized. Skillful facilitators guide teachers to recognize the unit storyline or arc of a lesson sequence before focusing on individual lessons. Then, they demonstrate how lessons work and build on one another, and they emphasize how learning should unfold. As part of this introduction, teachers view sample lessons or watch videos of lessons from a district where students have similar strengths and needs. They also spend time surfacing assumptions and beliefs about how to teach their subject and how to engage students in grade-level content.

Then, teachers try the curriculum materials out for themselves. Often this experience uses an immersion model of professional learning where teachers are given the opportunity to participate in lessons using a learner lens. Led by a facilitator, teachers become learners and are asked to consider their students' perspectives as they engage in the lesson. This sometimes means they temporarily set aside their subject-matter expertise as teachers. By experiencing the curriculum themselves, teachers can anticipate the questions and ideas their students might voice in class and see how expert facilitation can guide discussion toward a learning goal. This experience enriches teachers' understanding of the curriculum and can deepen their content understanding as well by prompting them to approach their subject from an unfamiliar starting point. They explore the questions, misconceptions, and discoveries most likely to shape their students' thinking and work.

Following this experience, teachers return to their usual vantage points to reflect on their experiences as learners and revisit their initial assumptions about instruction and the new curriculum. They collaborate with colleagues who teach the same subject or grade to prepare to use the instructional materials in their classrooms.

Once teachers move into the ongoing implementation phase and begin using the curriculum on a regular basis, learning designs shift to a focus on individualized support from teacher leaders or coaches. They participate in ongoing opportunities to reflect with colleagues who teach the same subject or grade band. What results is a routinized process of studying, planning, rehearsing, and reflecting on the units and lessons before they teach them. Teachers continually enhance their expertise and eventually take on roles as teacher leaders, where they coach new colleagues through the different stages of learning to use new instructional materials.

Reflect on this:

1. What changes about the design of professional learning when teachers are provided opportunities to experience the curriculum themselves?

2. Why do you think using an immersive learner lens is critical in curriculum-based professional learning?

3. How are student- and teacher-facing instructional materials used in learning designs for curriculum-based professional learning?

Putting Learning Designs to Work

This approach to learning designs (see Table 6.1) represents three major shifts from the way most professional development occurs:

- **Shift teachers' perspectives:** Rather than tell teachers about a curriculum, let them experience it for themselves. Using a learner lens can help teachers not only trust that student-led discussions can be productive but also anticipate questions and ideas that will likely surface.

- **A mirror image:** Teachers should engage in the same sort of inquiry and reflection that they will have students engage in. In curriculum-based professional learning, teacher learning is the focus and the goal, so each activity engages teachers in discussion and reflection about what contributed to their development.

- **Build homegrown expertise:** Curriculum-based professional learning extends past the early use of a new curriculum. Veteran teachers participate in ongoing opportunities to reflect with colleagues and support each other in preparing to teach future units and lessons. As new teachers are hired, they too will need support to understand how to use the school's curriculum. Schools and districts will benefit from investing in teacher leaders and other instructional leaders to provide early use immersive learning opportunities and ongoing coaching.

TABLE 6.1 CHANGING EMPHASES: Learning Designs	
Learning designs are a Functional Design feature that encompasses the following changes in emphases:	
LESS EMPHASIS ON	**MORE EMPHASIS ON**
Launching new initiatives each year	Focusing on curriculum implementation over multiple years
One-size-fits-all approach to planning professional learning support for the use of new instructional materials	Different learning designs that support teachers at different phases of implementation using new instructional materials
One-shot professional learning that takes place in the summer to learn how to use new instructional materials	Professional learning that is spread out during the school year to support the early use of new instructional materials
Relying on outside experts to lead curriculum-based professional learning	Building the capacity of teacher leaders to share responsibility for leading curriculum-based professional learning
Trainings for teachers on new instructional materials	Learning experiences that mirror the instructional approach students will experience using new instructional materials

Be

Beliefs

Examining Beliefs About Curriculum and Instruction

"If you think about it, the teacher has a lot of control. The teacher is with the students every day. The teacher is who determines what lesson gets put in front of students. And so, if you don't build teacher buy-in and leadership, and if teachers, in their hearts, don't believe that this is important and that students can learn at this rigorous level, then the instructional shifts are just not going to happen."

—Sarah Johnson, Chief Executive Officer Teaching Lab

Traditionally, students have been expected to recall facts and master skills. Critical thinking has mostly been reserved for enrichment after a foundation of knowledge is secured. As a result, many teachers spend their limited time drilling down to the basics and ensuring that students memorize everything they need to know. Preparation and lesson

FUNCTIONAL DESIGN FEATURES

planning focus on teacher-led presentations that engage and efficiently relay content to students so that information will stick. Often, students who are remediated are members of underserved populations. When educators are wed to the belief that these students cannot be challenged with higher-order thinking, they become barriers to achieving equity.[4]

By contrast, college- and career-ready academic standards and high-quality instructional materials put student thinking front and center. Students are asked to think rather than memorize, to reason rather than imitate. Lessons look and feel unfamiliar—students imperfectly interpret and apply independent reasoning, and group work and discussion nudge them toward better answers and content mastery. Teaching becomes a process of provoking students to think critically and guiding them along productive paths to reach intended outcomes. Teachers have to let go of leading and give students a different type of support while keeping pace with academic expectations.

Beliefs address teachers' ideas and assumptions about how to teach specific content, how students learn the same content, and how high-quality instructional materials provide productive ways to support student learning.

Just as this type of curriculum prioritizes student thinking, curriculum-based professional learning prioritizes teacher thinking. Both the curriculum and the professional learning ask teachers to examine their beliefs about what effective instruction looks like and their role in the classroom.

Beliefs are often addressed through two phases.[5] The first is catalyzed by a disruptive experience, something that contradicts the tenets underlying teachers' daily practice or their assumptions about what they or their students can do. This experience can take different forms, depending on the teacher or school, such as taking a learner perspective and participating in a lesson, observing a lesson taught to students who resemble those in a teacher's classroom or school, or seeing a colleague use new instructional materials and experience outsized gains in student learning. The goal is to promote cognitive dissonance—a state of discomfort that occurs when new information clashes with preexisting beliefs. These kinds of experiences lay the groundwork for self-reflection and conversations about current assumptions and beliefs and the impact they may be having on practice.

Then, teachers may benefit from time and space to reflect on this dissonance with their coaches and colleagues. Through reflection, they can make sense of new information and examine any deep-seated beliefs that have surfaced. This second phase involves small-group discussion, guided reflection, and detailed curriculum study. Through this reflective work, teachers can resolve the dissonance between certain long-held beliefs about teaching and learning and what the new curriculum requires.[6]

For example, science teachers often believe it is necessary to teach students specific vocabulary prior to engaging in inquiry-based investigations. Teachers have the belief that students need to know these definitions to successfully conduct investigations and analyze data. When science curriculum materials provide a different approach to instruction that introduces definitions later in a sequence of activities, teachers may want to modify the lessons and continue to preteach the vocabulary. In curriculum-based professional learning as teachers are experiencing instructional materials as intended, they might become uncomfortable with the approach. Only after teachers have observed or even tried using a new curriculum with their own students and they respond positively will teachers begin to reconsider this belief.

Without ensuring that teachers fully understand and buy into new paradigms of student learning and success, we can't expect them to embrace new curriculum. When curriculum-based professional learning is embedded in teachers' daily jobs and in curriculum reform, it deepens teachers' understanding of the instructional materials and minimizes their use of shortcuts and simplifications that can shortchange student learning.

Reflect on this:

1. Think of a time when you experienced cognitive dissonance related to your beliefs about effective teaching.

2. What was this experience like for you?

3. How were you able to resolve the dissonance?

Putting Beliefs to Work

This view of beliefs (see Table 6.2) represents three major shifts from the way most professional development occurs:

- **Rock the boat:** To kick-start new ideas, give teachers evidence of what works, and ask them what they think about it. A disruptive learning experience, such as putting on a student hat during a model lesson or seeing a lesson taught in an authentic setting, can launch a conversation on teachers' assumptions about instruction.

- **Reflect and resolve:** Reflection should be part of teachers' cycle of learning and rooted in their experiences. Channeling teachers' discoveries and discomfort into new practices and beliefs is a critical aspect of curriculum-based professional learning. Teachers need ongoing, job-embedded opportunities to work with their colleagues, resolve cognitive dissonance, and discuss, update, and clarify their thinking.

- **Seek clarity:** Discussions or reflections about beliefs often start with general statements of values, such as "All kids can learn." But they must go deeper than that. Individual teachers have built their belief systems over time, and they won't all need the same type of disruptive experience to prompt change. Learning experiences should be tailored to schools and teachers, and efforts to make meaning and resolve cognitive dissonance should be connected to teachers' own students. Facilitated conversations and well-chosen writing exercises can prompt teachers to think critically about their practices and students' experiences.

TABLE 6.2   CHANGING EMPHASES: Beliefs

Beliefs are a Functional Design feature that encompasses the following changes in emphases:

LESS EMPHASIS ON	MORE EMPHASIS ON
Inspirational keynote speakers intended to motivate and inspire	Learning experiences that promote cognitive dissonance
Learning experiences focused solely on new standards and deepening content knowledge	Learning experiences that surface beliefs about how content should be taught
What practices must change and how to use new instructional materials	Attention to cognitive-dissonance-resolving exercises that contextualize learning for educators' schools and classrooms
Limited access to high-quality educative instructional materials that address shifts in beliefs as well as practice	Broad access to high-quality educative instructional materials that address shifts in beliefs as well as practice
Personal reflections on beliefs and assumptions	Embedded discussions and reflections that address beliefs and assumptions throughout learning cycles and collaborative work

Opportunities for Deep Reflection and Feedback

"As teachers integrate this new curriculum into their practice, they do not need feedback that is evaluative. Teachers need a regular cadence of feedback that focuses on changes in practice and enhances implementation."

—Janise Lane, Executive Director of Teaching and Learning, Baltimore City Public Schools

Few people can learn in a vacuum—all but the most solitary creatures among us crave reflection and feedback on our work. Performance conversations contribute to each stage of the learning cycle for both students and adults. Without regular opportunities for teachers to reflect and receive feedback, their practice can plateau.[7]

Reflection and feedback call for facilitated time when teachers think about new instructional materials, receive input on how best to use them, examine student work and assessment data, and make changes to instructional practice in response.

High-quality instructional materials are designed to include moments of reflection and feedback to help students learn to develop, share, and act on insights from one another. Frequent assessments and student surveys give teachers timely, ongoing feedback about what students are experiencing and learning.

Similarly, high-quality curriculum-based professional learning embeds reflection and feedback in various forms, ranging from an explicit step in the learning cycle to a quick step back during learning activities with fellow teachers, coaches, and teacher leaders. Through reflection and feedback, teachers can examine and shift their beliefs, gain context for their work and experiences, and deepen their curriculum and content knowledge. These processes offer powerful opportunities to think and learn.

Reflection is introduced early and reintroduced frequently in the process of curriculum implementation. After teachers first encounter new instructional materials, they may be asked to reflect on their previous experiences and how they differ from this new type of teaching and learning. Individually and in small groups, teachers consider and articulate their strengths and weaknesses in light of the new materials, as well as their aspirations and intended outcomes for students.

FUNCTIONAL DESIGN FEATURES

These detailed conversations help teachers understand how to apply new instructional materials within the context of their school and how to use their knowledge of students' culture, needs, and interests to make lessons and materials more relevant and engaging. This approach also prompts teachers and instructional leaders to establish reflection as an ongoing priority. Time for reflection is then built into individual and team learning cycles to ensure that teachers actively reflect on their learning and application of new materials with students.

The types of feedback that lead to meaningful growth among teachers look nothing like letter grades. Feedback comes from a variety of perspectives and may be spoken or written. For example, a professional colleague, coach, or leader may offer specific, data-driven feedback based on shared definitions and understandings. When a coach or peer observes a lesson and raises questions, their feedback creates a foundation for conversations about goals for improved teacher practice and implementation of instructional materials.[8] Ultimately, the value of feedback is measured by the changes and improvements it prompts.

Curriculum-based professional learning also includes examining student work and assessment data to spur reflection and feedback. Collaboratively looking at student learning data from interim or summative assessments, as well as formative assessment opportunities embedded in daily lessons and units, provides teachers with direct evidence of student progress. Teachers benefit from examining different forms of student work together as they implement curriculum since it helps pinpoint concepts students are finding difficult and may uncover aspects of lessons that need revision. More informal data sources, including student responses to teacher questioning and exit tickets, may also provide insights into students' needs, challenges, interests, and opinions.

Another type of feedback comes from how students behave in class. Students provide teachers with feedback on instruction all the time. Those who are enthusiastic and engaged provide one type of obvious feedback, but disinterested students provide critical feedback, too. When students mentally check out of class, they may be signaling a lack of understanding, disinterest in what is taking place, or distraction by a personal challenge that needs addressing. They are telling their teacher that their connection is fraying and that something needs to change. All these sources of data can provide valuable feedback and fodder for reflection and learning for teachers using a new curriculum.

Putting Reflection and Feedback to Work

This view of reflection and feedback (see Table 6.3) represents three major shifts from the way most professional development occurs:

- **Trust the process:** Effective feedback lays the groundwork for teachers to recognize their strengths and weaknesses and commit to ongoing improvement. Teachers' confidence in observers, peers, instructional materials, and the processes they use affects the degree to which they embrace feedback and reflection. Observations by peers and seeing others teach can provide a common, shared experience that builds confidence in using new curriculum.

- **A broad look for evidence:** Feedback that leads to growth takes many forms. One type comes from coaches and peers. This type of feedback is bite-sized and grounded in shared definitions and metrics of success. Another type is based in how students engage with instruction. Are they participating, learning the material, and remaining connected to their classmates and the process of learning? Neither type of feedback is used to evaluate performance; rather, both serve to describe progress, diagnose challenges, and create a road map for greater success.

- **Observe and reflect together:** In years past, teachers were left to their own devices and provided feedback only during performance evaluations. Curriculum-based professional learning is less hierarchical and more constructive in its feedback processes. At each stage of the curriculum implementation process, teachers reflect individually and jointly on their instruction and the curriculum, both in facilitated conversations and sometimes individually. Observations and feedback distinct from formal performance evaluation are conducted by instructional leaders, coaches, and peers.

TABLE 6.3   CHANGING EMPHASES: Reflection and Feedback

Reflection and feedback are a Functional Design feature that encompasses the following changes in emphases:

LESS EMPHASIS ON	MORE EMPHASIS ON
Feedback and reflective practices used solely during the monitoring and assessment phases of the learning cycle	Feedback and reflective practices embedded in every phase of the teacher learning cycles
Feedback offered only in a supervisory relationship	Feedback given by supervisors, coaches, and peers
Feedback delivered only in an evaluative manner	Feedback and reflective practices used to promote growth and development
Feedback and reflective practices encouraged	Coaches and teacher leaders prepared to facilitate feedback and reflective practices

Addressing Concerns Through Change Management

"For any of us to be open to learning and receiving new ideas, we need to feel known, seen, and valued in the context of our own situation. This is why we have found 'shoulder-to-shoulder' learning to be the most effective path to change in practice."

—Emily Freitag, Cofounder and Chief Executive Officer, Instruction Partners

Curriculum implementation is complicated and takes time. Yet the pace of school remains—there's no postponing fourth-grade reading or seventh-grade math. Meanwhile, district- or school-level changes are meaningful only when they reach every classroom. That means teachers need careful support as they transition away from the instructional style they have developed and practiced and feel comfortable with while keeping pace with students' needs.

Change management addresses teachers' individual concerns and group challenges when implementing new instructional materials, including explicit opportunities to discuss and troubleshoot issues.

There are many approaches to change management. In the case of curriculum implementation, we are referring to the necessary processes for transitioning to using new instructional materials. Applying strong change management strategies and practices to curriculum-based professional learning can help teachers make these shifts. Successful change management starts with the knowledge that change isn't something that just happens—it's a process, not an event.[9] And it begins at the individual level; it is deeply personal and requires learning.[10] Learning something new always precedes change; otherwise, what is the motivation to try something new?[11]

In the past, schools and districts intent on replacing their curriculum tended to manage the process as a series of tasks culminating in a launch: pick a program, acquire materials, arrange for professional development, and tell staff when to start. This type of "top-down" change effort rarely results in substantive changes to classroom practice envisioned by the curriculum developers. Without securing teachers' buy-in, the materials may change, but daily instruction won't. And without supporting teachers to gain new perspectives and instructional skills, even the most passionate efforts are likely to fall short. What is needed is top-down support for "bottom-up" change.[12]

Consider our current understanding of how students learn best. We don't expect students to enthusiastically master polynomial equations or sonnets after hearing a lecture and re-creating what they were told. Instead, teachers provide multiple opportunities for students to construct their understanding of a new topic over time. Students interact with knowledge and ideas with growing levels of complexity. They demonstrate new knowledge and skills, reflect on what they don't yet know, and continue to deepen their learning.

Curriculum-based professional learning is rooted in a vision of teachers as learners. Much like their students, teachers benefit from multiple opportunities to explore new instructional materials. But they also are under constant pressure to ensure their students succeed, even as they replace trusted practices and familiar materials. Change management for curriculum implementation requires attention to teachers' attitudes and feelings about using new instructional materials, as well as their ability to use them and understanding how they are designed. The phases of curriculum implementation and the change process suggest that ongoing support provides a necessary foundation for lasting improvement.

Effective curriculum-based professional learning is grounded in a plan that supports both individual and organizational change. Learning experiences are designed and scheduled. Timelines are set and responsibilities clarified. And while careful attention is paid to detail, there is also a recognition that schools are complex organizations. At times, things may not go as smoothly as planned—which means that district leaders, principals, coaches, and professional learning designers and facilitators must draw from research-based tools and resources to support individuals and institutions to work through these challenges.

FUNCTIONAL DESIGN FEATURES

The Concerns-Based Adoption Model

"Change is not easy, and it happens through intentional learning—for educators and students alike. Adopting new curriculum materials and making the instructional shifts needed to accelerate learning and meet new standards may not always be comfortable. But with the right mindsets, mission, and systemic support, all teachers and students can make the leap."

—*Denise Glyn Borders, President and Chief Executive Officer, Learning Forward*

There are several approaches to change management. One, the Concerns-Based Adoption Model (CBAM),[13] has a substantial evidence base and has been widely used in many school change efforts. CBAM provides a framework and tools for understanding the change process and providing appropriate and timely support to individuals experiencing it. It includes three main components: Stages of Concern About the Innovation,[14] Levels of Use of the Innovation,[15] and Innovation Configurations.[16]

In applying this framework to curriculum reform and professional learning, we look to the Stages of Concern to chart teachers' shifting reactions and feelings and how to respond to them. The Levels of Use characterize typical behaviors as teachers' competence improves over time. Innovation Configurations represent the ideal vision of the implementation of new curriculum, with a richly detailed set of actions teachers will demonstrate.

Stages of Concern describe the affective, or personal, dimensions of any change (see Figure 6.1). There is an array of feelings, perceptions, worries, preoccupations, and moments of satisfaction for those engaged in substantive change. The personal side of change is important to understand because failing to address concerns can lead to resistance and rejection. The measure outlines multiple stages and describes the reactions, attitudes, or perspectives of an individual in each stage related to a specific change. Personal concerns must be addressed before educators are ready to discuss benefits of innovations for students. Identifying a person's concern can be a relatively easy process and can be collected in writing or through conversation. Leaders and learning facilitators capable of identifying an individual's stage of concern can offer appropriate learning and support to enable the person to move beyond it.

Levels of Use describe a set of behavioral profiles that distinguish different approaches to using an innovation such as new curriculum materials (see Figure 6.2). These stages progress from Nonuse to Renewal. Each has implications for how to facilitate change and for evaluating success of change efforts. Knowing an individual's Level of Use helps leaders identify the supports necessary for improving implementation.

FIGURE 6.1   Stages of Concern About the Innovation: Concerns-Based Adoption Model

Stage 6 Refocusing: The focus is on the exploration of more universal benefits from the innovation, including the possibility of major changes or replacement with a more powerful alternative. Individuals have definite ideas about alternatives to the proposed or existing form of the innovation.

Stage 5 Collaboration: The focus is on coordination and cooperation with others regarding use of the innovation.

Stage 4 Consequence: Attention focuses on impact of the innovation on students in their immediate sphere of influence. The focus is on relevance of the innovation for students; evaluation of student outcomes, including performance and competencies; and changes needed to increase student outcomes.

Stage 3 Management: Attention is focused on the processes and tasks of using the innovation and the best use of information and resources. Issues related to efficiency, organizing, managing, scheduling, and time demands are utmost.

Stage 2 Personal: Individuals are uncertain about the demands of the innovation, their inadequacy to meet those demands, and their role with the innovation. This includes analysis of their role in relation to the reward structure of the organization, decision making, and consideration of potential conflicts with existing structures or personal commitment. Financial or status implications of the program for self and colleagues may also be reflected.

Stage 1 Informational: A general awareness of the innovation and interest in learning more detail about it is indicated. Individuals seem to be unworried in substantive aspects of the innovation in a selfless manner such as general characteristics, effects, and requirements for use.

Stage 0 Awareness: Little concern about or involvement with the innovation is indicated.

From *Measuring Stages of Concern About the Innovation: A Manual for Use of the SoC Questionnaire* (p. 7) by G. E. Hall, A. A. George, and W. L. Rutherford, 1979, Austin: The University of Texas at Austin, Research and Development Center for Teacher Education.

FUNCTIONAL DESIGN FEATURES

FIGURE 6.2	Levels of Use of the Innovation: Concerns-Based Adoption Model
Users	**Level VI Renewal:** State in which the user reevaluates the quality of use of the innovation, seeks major modifications of or alternatives to present innovation to achieve increased impact on clients, examines new developments in the field, and explores new goals for self and the system.
	Level V Integration: State in which the user is combining their own efforts to use the innovation with related activities of colleagues to achieve a collective impact on clients within their common sphere of influence.
	Level IVB Refinement: State in which the user varies the use of the innovation to increase the impact on clients within the immediate sphere of influence. Variations are based on knowledge of both short- and long-term consequences for clients.
	Level IVA Routine: Use of the innovation is stabilized. Few if any changes are being made in ongoing use. Little preparation or thought is being given to improving innovation use or its consequences.
	Level III Mechanical Use: State in which the user focuses most effort on the short-term day-to-day use of the innovation with little time for reflection. Changes in use are made more to meet user needs than client needs. The user is primarily engaged in a stepwise attempt to master the task required to use the innovation, often resulting in disjointed and superficial use.
Nonusers	**Level II Preparation:** State in which the user is preparing for first use of the innovation.
	Level I Orientation: State in which the user has recently acquired or is acquiring information about the innovation and/or has recently explored or is exploring its value orientation and its demand upon the user and user system.
	Level 0 Nonuse: State in which the user has little or no knowledge of the innovation, has no involvement with the innovation, and is doing nothing toward becoming involved.

From Measuring Levels of Use of the Innovation: A Manual for Trainers, Interviewers, and Raters (pp. 171–195) by S. F. Loucks, B. W. Newlove, and G. E. Hall, 1975, Austin: The University of Texas at Austin, Research and Development Center for Teacher Education.

Innovation Configurations recognize that each implementer may not share the same vision for or understanding of the curriculum and as a result implementation by each may look very different. Innovation Configurations anticipate deviations that may occur across classrooms and spell out the most desirable practices. They break down key elements of the curriculum and provide rich detail of actions that progress to the ideal vision for implementation. Leaders can use Innovation Configuration maps to support and monitor individuals' progress in learning about and using the new instructional materials. They can serve as the basis for constructive feedback and future support. Innovation Configuration maps (for examples, see Figures 6.3 and 6.4) are growth-inducing tools, indicating where implementers are on the continuum toward the ideal and where they need help to advance their learning and performance.

FIGURE 6.3 Innovation Configuration on Use of Instructional Materials

Innovation Configuration

Use of Instructional Materials

EXPERT	EXPERIENCED	NOVICE	NOT EVIDENT
Teacher implements the instructional materials as intended by the developer. Teacher demonstrates an understanding of the instructional model used in the materials.	Teacher implements the instructional materials with a basic understanding of the instructional model used in the materials. Teacher may make "user-oriented" changes rather than student-centered changes in the materials.	Teacher selects certain activities from the instructional materials with little understanding of the instructional model.	Teacher uses the instructional materials as a reference but does not teach from them.

From "Innovation Configuration on Use of Instructional Materials" by BSCS Science Learning, November 2008.

FUNCTIONAL DESIGN FEATURES

FIGURE 6.4   Innovation Configuration on Learning Sequence in Instructional Materials

Innovation Configuration
Learning Sequence in Instructional Materials

	EXPERT	EXPERIENCED	NOVICE	NOT EVIDENT
FUNCTIONAL DESIGN FEATURES	Teacher understands the learning sequence in terms of the learning goals.	Teacher understands the learning sequence in terms of the learning goals.	Teacher partially understands the learning sequence in terms of the learning goals.	Teacher does not recognize the coherence of the learning sequence.
	Teacher modifies the learning sequence based on sound science conceptual development and in response to student work. Modifications promote student understanding of complex concepts.	Teacher teaches activities in a well-sequenced manner to promote student understanding of concepts but does not necessarily monitor and adjust based on student work.	Teacher teaches activities in an uneven sequence and in a manner that only partially helps students develop conceptual understanding.	Teacher teaches as if there were no structure for students to achieve the learning goals.
	Teacher designs/uses a learning sequence that demonstrates concepts, themes, and skills and the relationships between them. The learning sequence ensures that all students develop a deep understanding of core science concepts.	Teacher uses a learning sequence that demonstrates concepts, themes, and skills. The learning sequence supports an understanding of core science concepts for all students.	Teacher uses a loosely organized learning sequence. Teacher inconsistently demonstrates concepts, themes, and skills. The learning sequence supports an understanding of core science concepts for some students.	Teacher uses a sequence that is not organized and rarely demonstrates concepts, themes, and skills. The sequence rarely supports students' understanding of core science concepts.
	Teacher recognizes that a learning sequence occurs within a unit of instruction, not just a lesson sequence, and is willing to adjust the time allocation based on student feedback.	Teacher recognizes that a learning sequence occurs within a unit of instruction, not just a lesson sequence, and attempts to adjust the time allocation based on student feedback.	Teacher recognizes a learning sequence occurs within a lesson.	Teacher does not recognize the parameters of a learning sequence.

From "Innovation Configuration on Learning Sequence in Instructional Materials" by BSCS Science Learning, November 2008.

Reflect on this:

1. How might some of your concerns about adopting and implementing a new curriculum be addressed?

2. Think of your own experiences with adopting new curricula and/or instructional practices. Did you feel adequately prepared to embrace and ultimately master the requisite changes in practice? What supports might have been helpful in elevating your confidence level around the change?

3. Which of the three CBAM tools described earlier would have been most helpful to you in enacting the change, and why?

Putting Change Management to Work

This view of change management (see Table 6.4) represents three major shifts from the way most professional development occurs:

- **A process, not an event:** Change isn't the difference between before and after—rather, it's an ongoing disruption of thinking and doing. It requires adults to make and remake their knowledge, actions, and beliefs, which requires attention and energy over time. Important change happens over three to five years, not during a single launch period.[17]

- **Support people:** Change is disruptive. It requires adults to let go of old ways of doing things and recasts their experience and expertise as less relevant or in need of an update. Supporting curricular change means guiding teachers to come to grips with uncertainty. Firsthand experience seeing that new curriculum materials benefit students can focus teachers on the benefits of the new rather than the loss of the old.

- **Stay the course:** In the midst of change, adults often look to restore their equilibrium, including by backsliding into old ways of thinking and doing. Ongoing reflection and feedback can help teachers remain connected to the process of change. These experiences are rooted in instructional coaching and facilitated curriculum-based professional learning experiences that challenge teachers to review evidence on student learning and reexamine their beliefs.

TABLE 6.4   CHANGING EMPHASES: Change Management

Change management is a Functional Design feature that encompasses the following changes in emphases:

LESS EMPHASIS ON	MORE EMPHASIS ON
Change as an event	Change as a process that occurs over time
Decision makers and learning facilitators who ignore change management strategies	Decision makers and learning facilitators who apply change management strategies to curriculum implementation
Launching change efforts by lauding benefits for students	Linking change efforts to benefits and support for teachers
Treating everyone in the change process the same	Using the Concerns-Based Adoption Model (CBAM) to individualize support and accelerate implementation

Baltimore City Public Schools and ELA Curriculum

Baltimore City Public Schools refreshed its blueprint for successful teaching and debuted an updated logo conveying its ideals in June 2020. It's a circle composed of three equal parts: Prepare, Teach, and Perfect & Adjust. Reflection and feedback are on the same footing as planning and instruction.

That visual update went hand in hand with other big changes: In 2018–2019, Baltimore adopted Wit & Wisdom, an English language arts curriculum developed by Great Minds. The district also partnered with the New Teacher Center to develop curriculum-aligned coaching. Both the New Teacher Center and Great Minds supported instructional coaches and district leaders to provide teachers with high-impact, job-embedded feedback and opportunities for reflection.

"We believe that to shift educator mindsets and improve student outcomes, professional learning must be rooted in rigorous, curriculum-aligned professional learning that is paired with job-embedded instructional coaching and regular feedback cycles," said Desmond Blackburn, chief executive officer at the New Teacher Center.

Teachers worked in learning teams and received one-to-one coaching. They created videos of instruction that coincided with cycles of feedback, and they participated in group reflections aimed at helping them to understand the curriculum materials and meet students' diverse needs. They received personalized feedback grounded in the materials, advancing their knowledge and skillfulness with it.

Feedback for teachers was aligned to the curriculum and consistent from one observer to the next. "It's easy to bombard teachers with feedback," said Janise Lane, executive director of teaching and learning at Baltimore City Public Schools. The district's feedback protocol gives teachers time to internalize their coach's feedback—in other words, time to "perfect and adjust."

Reflect on this:

1. What contribution does reflection make to sense-making during professional learning?

2. What different types of feedback are needed for effective curriculum-based professional learning?

3. How can reflection and feedback be used to promote teacher collaboration and build trust?

Closing Thoughts

Curriculum-based professional learning has four Functional Design *Elements*: **Learning designs** engage teachers as learners using the same instructional materials their students will use; **beliefs** address teachers' ideas and assumptions about teaching and learning; **reflection and feedback** help teachers think about curriculum and adapt it to meet the needs of their students; and **change management** addresses teachers' individual concerns and use of new instructional materials to help monitor curriculum implementation efforts. The Functional Design *Elements* inform the planning and implementation of curriculum-based professional learning. Using these Functional Design features is central to the work professional learning designers, facilitators, and instructional coaches do to support curriculum-based professional learning.

In the two examples from the field, several of these *Elements* were present. Both Boston and Baltimore City Public Schools focused on shifting educators' mindsets and perspectives. They did this through their learning designs that surfaced teachers' beliefs, provided them with new experiences, and supported them with opportunities to reflect on what they were learning as they progressed through different phases of curriculum implementation. Boston used a learning design that involved immersive opportunities for teachers in the early use phase of curriculum implementation to experience the curriculum through both learner and teacher lenses. Baltimore City continued to support teachers as learners during the ongoing implementation phase through job-embedded feedback and opportunities for reflection as teachers worked with instructional coaches. Both examples used the Functional Design *Elements* to help change what teachers were thinking and change what they thought was possible. It is also important to notice how these examples used different models, time, and collective participation in conjunction with learning designs, beliefs, and reflection and feedback to support teachers through the phases of curriculum implementation.

Although the tools of change management were not included in these examples, the foundations for change management were addressed. Curriculum implementation efforts in Boston and Baltimore City focused on both individual and organizational change. Change begins at the individual level when teachers learn something new and are supported to try what they have learned in the classroom. This type of professional learning demands careful attention by designers, facilitators, and coaches about what is designed and how the design is working. And this is especially important when things may not go as smoothly as planned and require adjustments to the learning designs and processes for reflection and feedback. Schools are complex organizations and require careful attention while monitoring the phases of curriculum implementation. In addition to the Core, Structural, and Functional Design features, it is important to consider the necessary conditions at the system level for curriculum-based professional learning, which is the focus of the next chapter.

Some of the most interesting lessons learned during the COVID-19 pandemic apply to the Functional Design *Elements*. Learning designs were translated to a new remote reality. While the goals for immersive and ongoing implementation support remained the same, many of the delivery strategies had to adjust. Immersive experiences balanced Zoom fatigue by spreading sessions over several days while continuing to prioritize teachers wearing learning hats. More classroom videos in contrast to direct observations were used to promote reflective conversations. New online learning tools made it possible to engage as well as track participation of adult learners. Beliefs and assumptions were regularly tested as teachers prepared to use high-quality instructional materials in their Zoom classrooms, which presented additional opportunities for learning and reflection. Professional learning communities became more important for planning, adapting, and rehearsing lessons for "prime time." Learners were no longer solely the students as families joined in and everyone provided powerful feedback to educators. Finally, long-term change management plans were useless as change management relied more on the tools to support day-to-day individual change and the emotions that accompany it and the skills needed to see it through. There is no doubt that COVID-19 pandemic experiences will continue to influence future planning for curriculum-based professional learning. Most likely, hybrid strategies will evolve that in the end strengthen the support given to educators for implementing high-quality instructional materials.

Where do you go from here?

- What more do you want to learn to put the Functional Design *Elements* into action?

- How do the Functional Design *Elements* contribute to successful professional learning?

- What are critical connections among the Functional Design *Elements*?

- What next actions will you pursue?

FUNCTIONAL DESIGN FEATURES

The Elements

of Curriculum-Based Professional Learning

Core
Design Features

Functional
Design Features

Structural
Design Features

Cu
Curriculum

CP
Collective
Participation

TL
Transformative
Learning

LD
Learning
Designs

Be
Beliefs

Mo
Models

Eq
Equity

RF
Reflection &
Feedback

CM
Change
Management

Tm
Time

The Essentials

Le
Leadership

Re
Resources

Co
Coherence

Essentials of Curriculum-Based Professional Learning

7

//

Where are you now?

- I am interested in reading more about the enabling conditions for curriculum-based professional learning.

- I am wondering if these conditions are supported by the system and school leaders in my own context.

- I am looking for ways to help build learning organizations that invest in high-quality instructional materials and support their implementation through curriculum-based professional learning.

- I am committed to helping system leaders and principals support teachers, contribute to a powerful vision for instruction, and enable the success of all students.

Sullivan County Schools and Teacher Leaders

In Sullivan County Schools, a rural district in eastern Tennessee along the Appalachian Trail, nearly four in ten students were identified as struggling readers. Those students couldn't complete grade-level tasks like analyzing a text, responding to a writing prompt, or answering questions using textual information. The district joined the LIFT network, short for Leading Innovation for Tennessee Education, to work with nonprofits TNTP and Tennessee SCORE, the State Collaborative on Reforming Education, to improve its reading curriculum and instruction.

It sounds like a top-down initiative run by outsiders—the sort that often falls short of expectations if teachers don't buy into it or engage in curriculum-based professional learning. But Sullivan County had built a corps of two dozen teacher leaders it called game-changers, and it turned to those teachers to help lead curriculum change.

Those teachers, along with district and school leaders, met to review and select instructional materials that were rigorous and relevant to students. They also questioned their underlying beliefs and assumptions about how students learn to read while reviewing reading research and how literacy was taught in Sullivan County.

"My epiphany came like a tornado rather than a gentle breeze when I was taught—through our collaboration with SCORE and TNTP—that we must build students' background knowledge while explicitly teaching foundational skills," said Robin McClellan, the district's supervisor of elementary education. "I realized, with great dismay, that our work didn't align with the research on how kids learn to read."

Sullivan County selected the Core Knowledge Language Arts curriculum for K–5, a content-rich curriculum with rigorous learning outcomes for student reading and writing. Teacher leaders piloted its implementation in the 2016–2017 school year, and then leaders and teachers set out to study and implement the curriculum together with support from SCORE and TNTP. District and school leaders conducted instructional walk-throughs and provided brief coaching sessions. They prioritized responding to teachers' feedback about the curriculum materials, pointing back to research, and they publicly celebrated teachers' work.

At the end of the pilot, the game-changers signaled their support for the Core Knowledge curriculum, which was rolled out in every school the following year. These teachers took on a new leading role: supporting and mentoring other educators to build knowledge and expertise. Meanwhile, district leaders continued to regularly collaborate with teachers to share their experiences during Board of Education meetings, and they highlighted shared leadership in communications with parents and the media. And student outcomes did improve: the portion of students considered at risk for reading failure declined from 38 percent in the fall of 2018 to 28 percent in the spring of 2019.

Reflect on this:

1. What role do teacher leaders play in your context, and how does it support curriculum implementation?

2. Sullivan County used a curriculum pilot to inform the district's rollout of new instructional materials. How does that resonate with your own experience? What might be costs and benefits of such an approach in your context?

3. How might teacher leaders or game-changers be utilized in subsequent years during the implementation and sustainability of a new curriculum?

This chapter describes three *Elements* we refer to as the **Essentials**—the necessary conditions at the system level for curriculum-based professional learning. These enabling conditions define expectations of system leaders and principals as well as opportunities for all others with responsibilities for supporting teachers and students. Each helps to build and sustain learning organizations, where ongoing investments in high-quality instructional materials and support for their implementation contribute to a powerful vision for instruction and success for all students.

In effective learning systems, strong **leadership** is represented by leaders who model and promote active learning for both children and adults. These leaders allocate adequate **resources** for curriculum implementation, including professional learning, making tough decisions about time, funding, assessments, and expert support. Such systems are characterized by **coherence**, with curriculum-based professional learning that both supports and is supported by other initiatives.

Leadership in a Learning Organization

"I see solutions that empower teachers and propel kids. I see the power of elevated expectations, structural strategy, collaboration, and the immeasurable value of leveraging the strengths, talents, and voices of teachers and leaders. We are propelling equity, equipping teachers with high-quality instructional materials, and enabling them to teach rather than gather and create."

—Robin McClellan, Supervisor of Elementary Education, Sullivan County Schools

THE ESSENTIALS

In education systems, we often view leadership through a "top-down" lens. But leadership looks different when schools operate as authentic learning communities. Leaders model and guide inquiry rather than simply transmitting expertise. They share responsibility and decision making to promote a common purpose and collective responsibility for student success.[1]

Leadership at a learning organization resembles teaching in an inquiry-based classroom. Like their students, teachers in such schools learn from their experiences, construct new understandings, and build on what they know about curriculum and instruction. Similarly, school and instructional leaders don't pretend to have all of the answers; instead, they ask questions, actively listen, and test out new ideas all the time. They model vulnerability and resilience, which promotes trust and encourages teachers to take risks, test assumptions, and break down old ways of thinking and doing.

In such schools, adults actively question, reflect, discuss, and build knowledge together.[2] Leaders visibly engage in learning alongside staff and colleagues. They engage teachers and instructional leaders in ongoing conversations to deepen their understanding of curriculum and improve instruction.

Leadership commits district, school, and teacher leaders to a shared vision for learning and instruction that applies to both children and adults, creates a culture of respect, and supports necessary risk-taking for curriculum implementation.

Effective leaders apply a constructivist approach to learning in their work. Constructivist leadership engages reciprocal processes that enable participants in an educational community to construct meanings that lead toward a common purpose about schooling.[3] Reciprocal processes are the mutual learning opportunities such as listening, questioning, reflecting, and facilitating that are used to build trust, encourage inquiry, test assumptions, and break down old ways of thinking. Constructivist leadership also focuses on meaning-making. Whether during professional learning sessions or leadership team meetings, leaders are responsible for creating the conditions for learning that advance new practices. This approach to leadership is critical to the successful implementation of curriculum-based professional learning.

Effective leaders are part of learning organizations that recognize learning as their core work.[4] Leadership transcends titles and often happens in teams, with individuals who have different skills and expertise working toward shared goals for student success. Decision-making responsibilities are entrusted to teachers and teacher leaders, whose work is anchored in a strong culture of inquiry, knowledge construction, reflection, and improvement.[5] The quality of a learning organization is a function of the quality of the conversations within it. Established structures and processes develop greater levels of leadership skillfulness that sustain an organization for its most important work, learning.[6]

When leaders see themselves as learners first, value their own learning, and visibly engage in learning with staff and colleagues, they are leading by example. When learning leaders deeply believe their colleagues and staff can learn what they need to know for all their students to do well, schools succeed. Highly effective leaders communicate consistently the vision for learning and teaching. They model a relentless pursuit for equity and excellence by prioritizing learning for all and creating a culture of respect.

Reflect on this:

1. How is this view of leadership consistent or inconsistent with your experiences?

2. Why do you think it's important for leaders to take a learner perspective in helping to support the needs of teachers using new instructional materials?

3. If leaders are not expected to have all the answers, what are they expected to know and be able to do?

Putting Leadership to Work

This view of leadership (see Table 7.1) rests on three big ideas:

*   **Leaders are learners:** Leaders don't have all of the answers; rather, they are continuously learning alongside their colleagues and teachers. They model learning activities like listening, questioning, and reflecting with colleagues, and their decisions prioritize support for teacher learning.

*   **Knowledge is constructed:** The process of learning is ongoing, as leaders and other adults build institutional and individual knowledge together. Leaders facilitate and listen as others compare past and current practices. They build trusting relationships that support honest, forward-looking reflection. These conversations create shared meanings and new habits and beliefs.

*   **A shared vision:** Leadership is rooted in shared ideas and understanding and transcends individual titles or roles. Through

THE ESSENTIALS

reflection, listening, study, and collaborative goal setting, teachers, coaches, and principals build a vision that guides professional learning and daily decisions.

TABLE 7.1   CHANGING EMPHASES: Leadership

Leadership is an enabling condition that encompasses the following changes in emphases:

LESS EMPHASIS ON	MORE EMPHASIS ON
Individual leadership capacity	Distributed leadership capacity
Superintendent- or principal-dependent leadership	Leaders surfacing from all roles in the organization and taking leadership action when appropriate
Interesting and memorable mission statements	Richly detailed vision statements that address learning and teaching and reference the importance of instructional materials and professional learning to support it
Building safe congenial relationships	Applying constructivist learning processes that facilitate authentic meaning-making and testing assumptions
Leaders advocating the importance of professional learning for teachers	Leaders advocating the importance of and engaging in curriculum-based professional learning with teachers
Leadership reserved for select groups of individuals	Broad-based leadership representation in all aspects of the work

Prioritizing Resources for Implementation

"When materials aren't open-source, it's really hard to build an integrated system because we don't have permissions— that's the power of open educational resources. The curriculum can play its true role as the center of the instructional vision, and everything can reinforce it."[7]

—Rebecca Kockler, Former Assistant Superintendent of Academic Content, Louisiana Department of Education

Curriculum-based professional learning takes commitment and resolve. Because change is an ongoing process, demands on time and school budgets are ongoing as well. Leaders who prioritize curriculum-based professional learning continually find the resources needed to support it. They also have a clear vision of curriculum-based professional learning that informs their decisions about how to allocate time, money, and professional effort. When leaders make decisions with this vision and these resources in mind, teachers are supported to study and use high-quality curriculum and instructional materials, participate in professional learning sessions with colleagues, and experience skillful coaching and facilitation.

Resources ensure that schools have adequate time and funding, high-quality standards-aligned instructional materials and assessments, access to experts, and the professional learning materials needed for sustainable implementation.

While resource considerations are not solely financial, money does matter. Engaging in curriculum-based professional learning requires investments in standards-aligned instructional materials and technical assistance providers to support their effective use. But it doesn't necessarily require a spending spree. Schools and districts can redirect current spending on textbooks and training sessions, for example, to purchase high-quality educative instructional materials or engage professional learning organizations to support curriculum implementation. States and systems can purchase standards-aligned curriculum materials, which on their own can accelerate student learning at low or no cost.[8] Alternatively, leaders can prioritize investments in curriculum-based professional learning over other budget categories. These can be tough choices for resource-constrained schools, but allocating resources to support curriculum-based professional learning can enable them to overcome inequities and drive results for teachers and students.[9]

In some cases, high-quality instructional materials are freely available online through Creative Commons licenses. Schools that adopt these types of materials can direct resources toward implementing them. Open educational resources, which are released under an intellectual property license that permits their free use, provide an alternative to commercially published proprietary curriculum materials. Some are digitally available in an editable format, enabling teachers to adapt them to meet their students' needs. While curriculum materials of this kind are freely available, it's important to remember that they

THE ESSENTIALS

do have associated costs—most districts still need printed materials, and teachers still need supplies like math manipulatives, trade books, and science equipment. They also need access to curricular expertise and time for curriculum-based professional learning.

Time is also a critical resource. Implementing new curriculum materials is an ongoing process; reserving extra days at the beginning or end of the school year to focus on implementation will not cut it. Successful curriculum implementation includes an early use phase that requires at minimum a couple of days and preferably an intense summer institute. Teachers benefit from additional time when learning to teach new units. The impact of curriculum-based professional learning is undermined when time is not allocated to implement it effectively. During the ongoing implementation phase dedicated time for collaborative learning and problem solving is required throughout the school year. To provide this, some leaders adopt a block schedule or another mechanism to establish weekly planning periods, enabling professional learning communities to meet during the school day. In setting expectations for those meetings, leaders might trim teams' agendas and refocus their time on curriculum.

Setting annual calendars and school day schedules gives leaders opportunities to consider expanding the number of professional learning days or building in after-school learning time for teachers as well as rearranging teacher schedules. During the pandemic, more organizations like the George W. Bush Institute called for a reexamination of the school year and school day.[10] Using these new designs, schools and districts can find the time necessary for the implementation of effective curriculum-based professional learning.

Leaders of professional learning are simultaneously visionaries and realists. They recognize the connection between resources and effective curriculum-based professional learning, so they both make efficient use of the resources they have and aggressively seek out additional resources to improve teaching and learning.[11]

In all these decisions, leaders are focused on building expertise in two main ways: (1) bringing in outside curriculum and professional learning facilitators to support implementation and (2) seeding homegrown expertise by identifying and supporting teacher leaders, instructional coaches, and school leaders. Both external and in-house experts can serve as champions and ambassadors for the curriculum, bringing new teachers up to speed and supporting veteran teachers as they refine and enhance their instruction.

Reflect on this:

1. How would you allocate the resources in your school or district to better support curriculum implementation efforts?

2. What types of outside expertise would your school or district benefit from that would improve curriculum implementation efforts?

3. In what ways could your school or district rethink the use of time to better support curriculum implementation efforts?

Putting Resources to Work

This view of resources (see Table 7.2) rests on three big ideas:

- **Honest accounting:** Curriculum-based professional learning takes a considerable amount of time, money, and effort. For professional learning to occur, those resources must be oriented toward a shared vision of curriculum and instructional improvement. Leaders must be clear with themselves and their colleagues about the extent of the resources required and be ready to make tough decisions about what to prioritize and what to put on the back burner. They also must clearly document the returns on these investments in terms of student progress.

- **Ongoing commitment:** The resources needed to support curriculum-based professional learning will fluctuate over time. Different resources are needed during curriculum launch and ongoing implementation, but the need for resources will never disappear. New teachers will need in-depth professional learning, and veteran staff members will benefit from booster shots of professional learning in addition to frequent opportunities for practice, data review, and refinement. These investments should be integrated and ongoing.

- **Audit for expertise:** Investments of time and money are ultimately investments in expertise, whether homegrown or external. Districts should take stock of available expertise in curriculum-based professional learning over time. Which teacher leaders are prepared to facilitate learning experiences? What resources are needed to build and maintain connections to

THE ESSENTIALS

external experts, such as curriculum developers, professional learning designers and facilitators, and researchers at local colleges and universities? Maintaining these talent pipelines and external relationships provides another important resource.

TABLE 7.2 CHANGING EMPHASES: Resources	
Resources are an enabling condition that encompasses the following changes in emphases:	
LESS EMPHASIS ON	**MORE EMPHASIS ON**
Selecting textbooks and other supplemental resources that are not integrated	Selecting full course curriculum with integrated assessments and tiered intervention supports
Curriculum-agnostic coaching support for teachers	Curriculum-specific coaching support for teachers
Curriculum procurement and professional learning services being siloed and purchased separately	Curriculum and professional learning services being integrated and purchased in tandem
Unclear return on investment in high-quality instructional materials and curriculum-based professional learning	Clear, well-documented return on investment in high-quality instructional materials and curriculum-based professional learning
Contracts with multiple partners for professional learning services that are fragmented and siloed	Working with multiple professional learning partners in an integrated and coherent fashion

Not All Resources Are Created Equal

It is just as easy to adopt a curriculum that is standards-aligned as one that is not—and curriculum matters. Fortunately, there are organizations working to increase the accessibility and identification of high-quality instructional materials and standards-aligned curriculum.

EdReports publishes free, comprehensive reviews of instructional materials on its website, with the goal of serving as a sort of Consumer Reports of instructional materials. It investigates materials prepared by traditional publishing houses as well as open-source instructional materials. A 2021 EdReports review found that 51 percent of published English language arts (ELA) materials and 44 percent of math materials were aligned to college- and career-ready academic standards.[12] In the 2021 review of materials regularly used in U.S. classrooms, EdReports found that just 25 percent of ELA materials and 40 percent of math materials were standards-aligned.[13] In other words, despite the availability of high-quality standards-aligned curricula, over 60 percent of schools and districts still use inferior materials.

Open educational resources have significantly expanded access to a variety of instructional materials and have been met with widespread demand. Instructional leaders and teachers from preschool through college can select relevant, standards-aligned materials to meet their students' needs, updating curriculum and instruction throughout a school year. Using open-source materials allows districts to invest more in curriculum-based professional learning and instruction and less in figuring out how to purchase or otherwise gain access to the necessary materials. It is important to note, though, that districts must still carefully vet open-source materials; just because something is freely available doesn't necessarily mean it is better.

One of the most broadly adopted open educational resources was launched by the New York State Education Department. The department used federal Race to the Top funds to create the EngageNY K–12 math and ELA curriculum, which includes individual lessons, teacher guides, and full instructional units with aligned professional learning resources. The math materials, also known as Eureka Math, align with the Common Core State Standards and have been downloaded more than thirteen million times by teachers in all fifty states.[14]

Louisiana took a similar path in developing its K–12 ELA Guidebook Units in partnership with LearnZillion. When the state couldn't find instructional materials to match new academic standards, leaders tapped a network of teacher leaders to develop new ones. ELA Guidebook Units and related professional learning resources are freely available under a Creative Commons license, and state education leaders report that most districts have opted to use them.[15] Use of the ELA Guidebook Units powers a focused, integrated vision for rigorous instruction and professional learning rooted in curriculum.

New open-source science materials also have been developed in response to the widespread adoption of new science standards. Twenty states have adopted the Next Generation Science Standards (NGSS), and another twenty-seven have adopted related new science standards. EdReports has begun reviewing widely used science instructional materials, and its initial review of middle school materials indicated that just one-sixth are aligned to the NGSS.[16] In response, initiatives like OpenSciEd—a collaboration between ten states, curriculum developers, and learning scientists supported by foundations (including Carnegie

THE ESSENTIALS

Corporation of New York, which launched the initiative)—are working to develop and field-test open-source K–12 science instructional materials and professional learning resources aligned with the NGSS.

In decades past, instructional materials were an all-in purchase at the school or district level. Boxes of textbooks and teachers' guides would crowd the main office, and teachers would gather in the auditorium for an introductory seminar. Students and teachers would work with those textbooks until the next adoption cycle. Open educational resources—and more specific definitions of high-quality instructional materials and curriculum-based professional learning—have shifted the priorities and the work.

Building Coherence With Curriculum Implementation

"When district leadership teams spend time thinking through and selecting standards-aligned instructional materials, strategic assessments, and meaningful professional learning, they no longer have to worry about what's happening across classrooms and schools. When they put the whole picture together, teachers and students have what they need to thrive."

—*Mora Segal, Chief Executive Officer, Achievement Network*

Teachers are motivated by boundless hopes for their students, but they regularly face a tough reality: you can't do it all in a day. Nimble instruction focuses students' time and energy where they matter most and engages learners at a sustainable level of effort. It pushes students to learn and grow but avoids cognitive overload.

Coherence aligns system and school policies, priorities, practices, and curriculum to a shared vision of learning and teaching.

Well-managed schools and systems operate on the same principle. There is no end to the running project list that energetic leaders or teachers have in their heads, and they run the constant risk of initiative overload. Successful schools operate with coherence, focusing efforts on a common purpose and selecting among competing priorities based on a central, driving mission. Their teachers collaborate as they strive toward excellence. They and their students work hard and maintain focus on what matters most.

Coherence thrives in systems where leaders embrace a shared vision, one in which rigorous, high-quality instructional materials and professional learning are central.[17] In these systems, a new curriculum or instructional practice doesn't come out of left field. It builds on what teachers are already working to achieve and clearly relates to an overall academic strategy. Teachers should not have to do cognitive backflips to figure out how new instructional materials will benefit their students.

Coherence also helps teachers and leaders decide how to use their time and energy. When schools operate with coherence, instructional and bureaucratic practices that don't align with their mission can be discontinued. Mixed messages and cross-purposes can be identified and brought into agreement. Coherence enables teachers and leaders to shift their efforts toward collaboration and professional learning experiences grounded in rigorous curriculum materials. It gives focus to cycles of learning and continuous improvement and shared accountability for progress.

Coherence gets at a fundamental truth about schools as learning organizations. Many organizations achieve alignment in policies and use instruction and assessments that make sense within their particular system.[18] But schools are most successful when they achieve a deep understanding of high-quality instructional materials and learning sequences for both students and adults. Coherent curriculum builds on ideas over time. Teachers create coherence when they use instructional materials to help students make connections between ideas, build on their prior learning, and apply what they have learned to solve problems.[19] Schools achieve coherence when they minimize distractions and promote the habits of mind that power inquiry among students, teachers, and leaders.[20]

THE ESSENTIALS

Reflect on this:

1. How coherent are the policies and practices that guide improvements in teaching and learning in your context?

2. How do decisions about resources and time impact and contribute to improving coherence?

3. Within your context, what would you like to change to make practices, priorities, and policies more aligned and coherent?

Putting Coherence to Work

This view of coherence (see Table 7.3) rests on three big ideas:

- **Share the vision:** Coherent schools have a compelling vision and mission that are evident in leaders' decisions, communications, and actions and create a common language for all school professionals. Explicit connections between a school's vision, language, and actions can sharpen decision making and illustrate the coherence that knits a learning organization together.

- **Ask why and how:** Successful schools prioritize strategies that promote curriculum-based professional learning and put them into action. In choosing among competing priorities, leaders select those that complement existing efforts and promote further success. They take concrete steps toward coherence rather than adopting policies that are only abstractly connected, working to clarify focus, cultivate collaborative cultures, secure accountability, and deepen learning.[21]

- **Go step by step:** Coherent curriculum-based professional learning helps teachers understand the structures underlying high-quality instructional materials. It guides teachers along a path to mastery, building their expertise through successive experiences and opportunities to reflect. By contrast, less coherent schools take a scattershot approach, solving problems as they occur. While professional learning can be responsive to teachers' evolving needs, its general trajectory should conform to a learning progression grounded in the curriculum.

TABLE 7.3   CHANGING EMPHASES: Coherence

Coherence is an enabling condition that encompasses the following changes in emphases:

LESS EMPHASIS ON	MORE EMPHASIS ON
Teachers communicating very different understandings regarding a common district vision for learning and teaching	Teachers communicating with similar words and feelings regarding the district vision for learning and teaching
School systems attempting to implement multiple initiatives to improve curriculum, instruction, and assessment	School systems focusing their instructional improvement efforts on curriculum implementation and curriculum-based professional learning
Teachers using a variety of instructional resources to create their own lessons and units	Teachers using high-quality full-course instructional materials to implement units and lessons
Creating a scope and sequence of topics that are modular and stand-alone instructionally	Developing a scope and sequence of units based on learning progressions that build on and connect ideas with each other
Policies that define coherence	Processes that build coherence

Caldwell Parish School District and Coherent Curriculum Implementation

Not too long ago, teachers in Caldwell Parish School District in Louisiana were giving a lot of lengthy tests. District policy required students to have two dozen test grades to track their progress over the year. While such data can be helpful, the tests took up a lot of class time—up to one full day each week. Students in the small, predominantly low-income district were struggling to meet grade-level standards in English, and teachers were constantly busy with planning, administering, and grading tests.

The district needed to refocus everyone's time on more rigorous teaching and learning to help students meet grade-level standards for reading and writing. So district leaders partnered with Achievement Network, a not-for-profit organization dedicated to achieving educational equity through great teaching and leadership, and together they tackled the tests. Achievement Network provided professional

THE ESSENTIALS

learning on what makes a quality standards-aligned assessment so that teachers could identify useful assessments that were already part of the ELA Guidebook Units they were using. Achievement Network also worked with school leaders to understand how teachers could meet the district's grading requirements without introducing new assessments from outside the curriculum. As a result of these efforts, testing decreased, and classes gained seven and a half days of instructional time over the course of a school year.

That was the first in a three-phase process of change. In the second, the district set a clear vision for instruction and professional learning. With support from Achievement Network coaches, leaders and teachers articulated goals, a theory of action for strategies to achieve them, and a plan for professional learning rooted in the ELA Guidebook Units. As a result, the goals for professional learning time were streamlined from ten down to just two, and the number of days teachers spent on curriculum-based professional learning increased from three to ten over the course of a school year. These changes gave teachers the time and support they needed to deepen their understanding of the content, how students learn that content best, and how to use the curriculum materials to accelerate learning.

Finally, in the third phase, the curriculum materials were implemented in classrooms. This work established a strong foundation for shifts in teachers' instruction, and both the district and Achievement Network noted that the majority of teachers used the instructional materials as intended. Now, 100 percent of students in Grades 6, 7, and 8 consistently engage with grade-level texts. And teachers, rather than spending their time searching for standards-aligned materials, are able to focus on refining their instruction to meet students' needs.

"Coaching conversations become so much deeper when you don't have to worry about what's being put in front of students," said Nicki McCann, superintendent of Caldwell Parish School District. "We no longer have to worry about the materials that teachers have in front of them. We know they are teaching with high-quality instructional materials and that they understand the importance of why the curriculum is put together in the way that it is."

Reflect on this:

1. Which *Elements* of curriculum-based professional learning were aligned to create coherence in Caldwell Parish's implementation of the ELA Guidebook Units?

2. Based on your experience, what would you prioritize to create coherence in curriculum implementation and associated professional learning?

3. How does coherence impact the ability to sustain curriculum implementation efforts and improve student learning at scale?

Closing Thoughts

Curriculum-based professional learning requires three Essential *Elements* that are necessary conditions at the system level for effective curriculum implementation: **leadership** from leaders who model and promote active learning for both students and adults; **resources** for curriculum implementation and professional learning; and **coherence** that both supports and is supported in systems by connecting curriculum implementation and professional learning efforts to other initiatives. These enabling conditions define the expectations of system leaders and school principals for supporting teachers. When taken together, the Essentials provide a backbone for building infrastructure, integrated support, and ongoing sustainability.

We see in the two examples from the field how paying attention to the Essentials *Elements* of curriculum-based professional learning is critical for successful implementation. Sullivan County Schools' development and use of teacher leaders was instrumental in helping inform the district's rollout of a new ELA curriculum. Often districts use pilots to inform curriculum implementation decisions. Sullivan County selected the Core Knowledge Language Arts curriculum and developed a cadre of teacher leaders to lead the implementation in classrooms. These teacher leaders also served as mentors as teachers across the district learned how to use new instructional materials that embodied a different approach to instruction. School and district leaders also used walk-throughs and coaching sessions to support their implementation efforts.

In Caldwell Parish School District, we see how connecting assessment practices with curriculum implementation and professional learning initiatives helped integrate their work and improve teachers' use of new instructional materials. This example of creating more coherence in ELA instructional systems was accomplished by focusing on three phases of work: curriculum-embedded assessments, planning professional learning aligned with a clear vision for instruction supported by the new instructional units, and learning to implement the curriculum materials in classrooms.

THE ESSENTIALS

Both examples relied on leaders taking a learner perspective to lead, allocating resources focused on curriculum and professional learning, and keeping a focus on learning and teaching to build coherence within systems. Combined with the other *Elements*, the Essentials create the necessary conditions to transform teaching through curriculum-based professional learning. In the next chapter, we focus on putting the *Elements* into action and provide recommendations for school and system leaders; teachers and school-based coaches; and professional learning providers, curriculum developers, and district curriculum coordinators.

The Essential *Elements* were critical as school systems and educators made their way through the unprecedented challenges of the COVID-19 pandemic. System leaders ultimately determined the priority they would place on maintaining course toward the instructional vision and the support teachers needed to ensure equity and excellence for all students. Systems with high-quality curricula in place recognized the benefit of a coherent program and the importance of allocating resources and support to sustain it.[22]

Several systems recognized the absence of high-quality curricula was forcing teachers to scramble for teaching materials, which resulted in an incoherent program of studies for many students. Some made the switch during the pandemic, and others adapted the curriculum they had. Unfinished learning from the first year of the pandemic meant teachers more than ever needed guidance on what to prioritize and how to scaffold instruction so all students could be successful with grade-level curriculum materials. Unprecedented resources were available to states and school systems to address student needs, and many districts allocated those dollars to hire additional staff to support teachers and students with these needs. Lessons remain to be learned on which actions produced the greatest impact for educators and students.

Where do you go from here?

- What more do you want to learn to put the Essential *Elements* into action?

- How do the Essential *Elements* create the enabling conditions for curriculum-based professional learning?

- What are critical connections among the Essential *Elements* that enable successful professional learning?

- What next actions will you pursue?

Elements in Action

Roles and Responsibilities

8

//

Where are you now?

- I am interested in reading more about the roles and responsibilities required for effective curriculum-based professional learning.

- I am wondering how well my organization's or system's current role expectations align with the recommendations in this chapter.

- I am open to rethinking priorities for myself and others responsible for successful curriculum implementation.

- I am committed to identifying future professional learning priorities based on rethinking roles and responsibilities.

We have introduced Chapters 1–7 with stories of how educators across the United States are investing in curriculum-based professional learning. In this final chapter, we hope to help you write your own school or district story. We focus on the roles and responsibilities of the people who are essential to the success of curriculum-based professional learning. We offer suggestions grounded in the research as well as the stories we shared and countless others we have studied. We share these ideas at a time of unique challenges and opportunities affecting education. Schools around the world are grappling with unprecedented disruption due to the COVID-19 pandemic and will be working to help students make up for unfinished learning opportunities and teaching time for years to come. As ever, though, what will have the greatest influence on student outcomes is the quality of teaching and the instructional materials used to engage students in learning. Efforts to broaden access to high-quality teaching and curriculum materials belong at the top of every system's improvement agenda.

We need to accept that teachers are poorly served by traditional approaches to professional learning. Professional development programs have not had substantial positive impacts on teacher performance or student outcomes, and teachers often view them as compliance exercises with little relevance to their work. Still, teachers haven't given up on professional learning, at least not in theory. And they want to get more out of it.[1] They are curious about their work and committed to their students. And when we ask teachers what they want, the answer is clear: the instructional materials, skills, and understanding they need to meet student needs and rigorous standards for student achievement.

We have the knowledge and tools to help. A strong evidence base shows that high-quality instructional materials accelerate student learning and that their impact grows even larger when teachers participate in curriculum-based professional learning.[2] Yet in too many cases, instruction is poorly aligned to the research on learning, and a wide gap remains between traditional teacher professional development and what is needed to teach well with high-quality instructional materials. These differences are most stark in classrooms serving students of color, who have far less access to rigorous curriculum and inquiry-based instruction than their peers.

Putting high-quality instructional materials and curriculum-based professional learning at the core can help us meet the challenges of the moment and continue to drive improvements in teaching and learning that reach all students. We can capitalize on the investments states and systems have already made in adopting college- and career-ready standards and the resources the federal government offers to support schools by better connecting teachers with curriculum developers and professional learning providers. In providing these supports, we can give teachers what they so clearly want and what research and evidence from the field indicate they—and their students—need.

In the remainder of this chapter, we focus on the target audience for this book—teachers, school-based coaches, professional learning providers, curriculum developers, and district curriculum coordinators, as well as school and system leaders. These recommendations help to translate the big ideas found in each chapter into the day-to-day actions that can help to propel this important work forward.

These stakeholder groups are providers and recipients of the pressure and support that accompany the level of change required to successfully execute curriculum-based professional learning. We organize these roles into three groups and address each one through the *Elements*. We offer this structure because we recognize that readers may identify with one group and want to start by reading about their role and responsibility and then turn to the other groups. Ultimately, how these play out will differ by context; however, the results could be similar if the goals are the same: ensuring students' access to educators who use high-quality instructional materials and receiving the support to implement new curricula effectively with all students to achieve outstanding results.

Reflect on this:

1. Where are efforts to broaden access to high-quality teaching and curriculum in your system's priorities?

2. Which roles and responsibilities are currently key to implementing your district's curriculum?

3. To what degree do you agree with and have data to support or refute the following: "When we ask teachers what they want, the answer is clear: the instructional materials, skills, and understanding they need to meet student needs and rigorous standards for student achievement."

The *Elements* are the expectations and accordant actions that school and district leaders, curriculum developers, and teacher development organizations take to promote and design curriculum-based professional learning (see Figure 8.1). They include:

- Core Design features, which focus on the purpose of curriculum-based professional learning

- Functional Design features, which shape teachers' experiences

- Structural Design features, which describe parameters and settings

Elements may be used in different combinations depending on what individuals and organizations need at different times. But all curriculum-based learning rests on **the Essentials**—expectations for system and school and leaders that nurture growth and change.

FIGURE 8.1 • The *Elements*

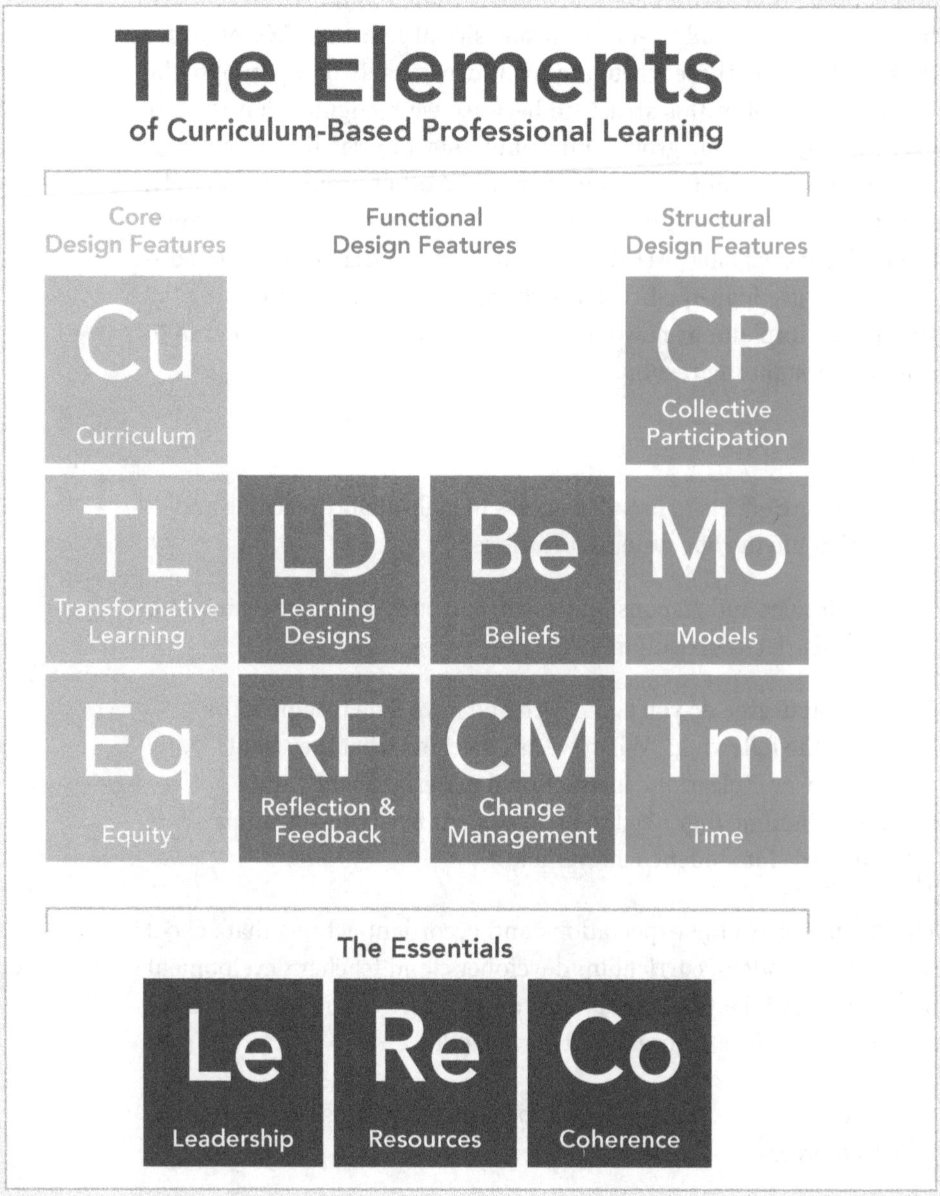

The Elements
of Curriculum-Based Professional Learning

Core
Design Features

Functional
Design Features

Structural
Design Features

Cu
Curriculum

CP
Collective
Participation

TL
Transformative
Learning

LD
Learning
Designs

Be
Beliefs

Mo
Models

Eq
Equity

RF
Reflection &
Feedback

CM
Change
Management

Tm
Time

The Essentials

Le
Leadership

Re
Resources

Co
Coherence

Roles and Responsibilities

Teachers and School-Based Coaches

We begin with those closest to the classroom including teachers and school-based coaches. Teachers may have formal leadership roles as a learning team facilitator, grade level or department chair, mentor, or cooperating teacher. Teachers may also contribute to the necessary changes through their contributions on curriculum selection or adoption committees. Most importantly, how teachers plan daily lessons and units allows everyday opportunities to put the *Elements* into action. School-based coaches working specifically at the school level have similar opportunities in their day-to-day interactions with teachers as well as their reporting and feedback responsibilities to supervisors. Many of the recommendations have applicability to both teachers and school-based coaches.

Putting Core Design
Elements Into Action

- Develop deep expertise in your disciplinary content and the *curriculum* to teach it and in the instructional materials used with students.

- *Transform learning* by assessing and clarifying beliefs and assumptions about teaching, learning, curriculum, and students on an ongoing basis.

- Promote *equity* by maintaining high expectations for students and using understanding of students' communities, cultures, racial and ethnic backgrounds, strengths, and interests to employ culturally responsive teaching strategies.

Your expertise as an educator is the number-one predictor of your students' success. Make a commitment to your discipline and *curriculum* your highest priority for professional learning. Be open to *transformational learning*. New instructional materials may challenge your current beliefs and assumptions regarding how you have approached teaching and learning in the past. Be aware of when your beliefs may prevent you from trying something new, and give yourself permission to test them. Try new ways of teaching to see the impact on students. Seek and use educative curriculum materials that provide support for scaffolding instruction and help all students do grade-level work. Immerse yourself in these types of resources and be prepared to have all students benefit from your expectations. Deep understanding of high-quality instructional materials enables one to advance *equity by* appropriately adapting to students' interests and using culturally responsive teaching strategies to adapt plans to advance students' success.

Putting Functional
Design *Elements*
Into Action

- Be open to *learning designs* that ask you to engage with a learner perspective.

- Examine your *beliefs and assumptions* throughout the learning process.

- Commit to ongoing *reflective practice* as well as seeking *feedback* and support from peers, coaches, and supervisors throughout the curriculum implementation process.

- Contribute to and use *change management* tools, including innovation configuration maps aligned with shifts in teaching practices supported by high-quality instructional materials, to guide improvement efforts.

Effective *learning designs* mirror the learning experiences for adults and students. Taking the perspective of a student learner promotes a deeper understanding of the instructional experiences intended for the classroom. This perspective also supports an examination of your *beliefs* and assumptions. Confusion or doubt may accompany experiences when you are asked to do something different from what is more familiar and comfortable. Remind yourself this is a natural and necessary part of the change process. Practicing *reflection* and seeking *feedback* contribute to processing and deepening new learning. While you are the expert in your classroom, there is inherent value in the perspectives and insights of others. Do not hesitate to seek it. Developing a deeper understanding of the *change management* tools described earlier will help you navigate the challenges of learning to use instructional materials that support new ways of teaching and identify helpful strategies to address these shifts in practice.

Putting Structural Design
Elements Into Action

- Hold yourself and others accountable for meaningful *collective participation* in learning.

- Develop knowledge of the benefits of various *models* of learning and engage as appropriate to strengthen curriculum implementation.

- Document the impact of *time* spent on curriculum-based professional learning for your practice and for students.

First and foremost, assume collective responsibility for all students served by members of your learning community. Learn and use the *collaborative structures* most appropriate for the different phases of curriculum implementation that will best guide you toward intended learning outcomes. Having this knowledge and expertise prepares you to raise questions or concerns when professional learning is not designed and executed to achieve the intended results. It positions you to benefit more from curriculum-based professional learning. Take advantage of different *models* to structure adult learning experiences and support curriculum implementation, such as professional learning communities, coaching, study groups, and co-teaching. Approach each learning experience with an expectation to learn deeply and act swiftly. Be open to recognizing when the expertise to address an issue does not reside within the group and an outside perspective is needed to further growth and development. Keep notes and be prepared to share how individual and system investments including *time* in curriculum-based professional learning are impacting you, your colleagues, and your students. Be an advocate for curriculum-based professional learning with parents and other key decision makers.

Putting Essential
Elements Into Action

- Exercise *leadership* by contributing to and championing a vision for teaching and learning supported by curriculum-based professional learning.

- Be advocates and good stewards of professional learning time and *resources* and hold peers and facilitators to the same standards.

- Promote *coherence* by limiting the use of supplementary materials to those that are clearly aligned with the vision for teaching and learning embedded in core curriculum.

Teachers and school-based coaches have many formal leadership opportunities, including school-based leadership teams and district curriculum committees, to influence the instructional vision for a school or system. Once these are established, all teachers may exercise formal and informal *leadership* by advocating for adequate *resources* and professional learning grounded in district curriculum and high-quality instructional materials adopted to support it. This alignment of vision, priorities, and action positions teachers to be able to experience and explains a curricular *coherence* that transcends grade levels and courses.

Reflect on this:

1. Which *Elements* are most critical for teachers to understand?

2. How are teachers prepared for their roles and responsibilities in relation to the *Elements*?

3. How should expertise in the *Elements* influence the selection of teachers for other leadership opportunities?

Roles and Responsibilities

Professional Learning Providers, Curriculum Developers, and District Curriculum Coordinators

Curriculum-based professional learning is a team effort. Professional learning providers, curriculum developers, and district curriculum coordinators are pivotal to connecting high-quality instructional materials with teachers and students. These professionals are in many schools and systems working in specific curricular areas or broadly across disciplines as supervisors or coaches. Some of these professionals work for organizations that partner with schools and systems to support the implementation of high-quality instructional materials. Whether working directly or through contractual arrangements with schools or systems, these individuals have substantive opportunities to advance implementation of the *Elements*. Professional learning providers and curriculum developers play a tremendous balancing act as they often recognize the huge responsibilities that must be accomplished without any formal authority. Each decision curriculum coordinators and professional learning providers make has potential to strengthen or fragment the ongoing learning and development of classroom teachers and their students.

Putting Core Design
Elements Into Action

- Anchor professional learning in district *curriculum* and high-quality instructional materials.

- Promote *transformative learning* by creating experiences that involve examining beliefs, assumptions, perceptions, and practices.

- Prioritize *equity* by helping teachers build connections between instructional materials and the culture, context, race, and ethnicity of their students.

Grounding professional learning in the instructional materials that teachers are asked to use with students addresses teachers' desire for relevant and timely professional learning. This requires curriculum developers to work with professional learning providers to gain a solid foundation in the *curriculum* and how to use high-quality instructional materials to develop pedagogical content knowledge and demonstrate teaching strategies embedded in them. You can't fake your way through curriculum-based professional learning. And if you attempt to do so, it's the teachers and students who suffer. Similarly, professional learning providers create *transformative learning* opportunities that ask participants to examine their beliefs and assumptions to prepare for potentially substantive changes to their practice. Educative curriculum materials often provide guidance to teachers on connecting lessons to student conceptions and sometimes misconceptions. Curriculum-based professional learning provides deeper understanding and appreciation of this guidance and prepares teachers to appropriately adapt curriculum to the context, needs, and interests of students. Effective use of curriculum materials promotes *equity* through culturally responsive teaching and access for all students. Throughout the COVID-19 pandemic, these educators played key roles in guiding essential decisions regarding teaching to make up for lost learning time and approaches for scaffolding instruction to keep students on grade level.

Putting Functional Design *Elements* Into Action

- Employ *learning designs* that introduce teachers to new curricula and reinforce their use through experiences that mirror the instructional approaches they will use with students.

- Apply research on how to shift *beliefs* and embed opportunities for cognitive dissonance and its resolution in professional learning.

- Embed multiple approaches to *feedback and reflection* throughout the learning designs, models, and change process.

- Develop expertise, guide development, and use *change management* tools to provide feedback and support during curriculum implementation. Individuals and organizations change at different paces. Expertise in applying change management tools will support and accelerate the process.

Functional Design *Elements* support the *learning designs* that prioritize experiences for teachers that mirror the instructional approaches they are expected to use with students. Ensuring teachers take a learner perspective and experience lessons they will use with students helps solidify understanding and commitment to the instructional vision offered by high-quality curricula. Meaningful changes in practice precede changes in *beliefs* and ultimately changes in student achievement. Providing multiple opportunities for teachers to observe and experience new instructional materials can lead to the cognitive dissonance that often precedes an examination of beliefs and assumptions. Leveraging *reflection and feedback* processes can contribute to this as well. Both come in multiple forms and promote learning and development throughout the curriculum implementation process. Formal and informal student assessment data provide insights into student progress, and reflection promotes thoughtful consideration of how best to respond to the data. Integrating such learning opportunities throughout the entire curriculum implementation process is important to sustaining momentum essential for lasting change. Individuals and organizations change at different paces. Expertise in developing and applying *change management* theory and tools including Stages of Concern surveys, Innovation Configuration maps, and Levels of Use interview protocols can help support and accelerate the different phases of the curriculum implementation process.

Putting Structural Design *Elements* Into Action

- Advise and guide system and school leaders to establish collaborative learning teams by grade and content area and build structures and protocols that advance *collective participation*.

- Develop expertise and apply learning *models* as appropriate throughout the different phases of curriculum implementation to provide ongoing support.

- Support the development of change management plans that recognize and allocate the essential *time* needed for curriculum implementation.

Curriculum-based professional learning is designed specifically for each phase of the curriculum implementation process from initial launch, to early use, ongoing implementation, and finally sustainability. Change management plans are essential to developing a shared understanding and support for the time and processes required to implement new curriculum effectively. Being an expert in developing such plans increases your value to the system as well as the potential of your work having its intended impact. *Collective participation*, *models*, and *time* are foundational to the success of each learning experience in the process. *Collective participation* promotes shared commitment and responsibility for successful application of curricula and the impact on students. *Models* of learning are applied according to intended outcomes. Intensive immersion experiences are key to successful curriculum launches as well as when new units and instructional materials are introduced throughout the first year of implementation.

Professional learning providers working with district curriculum coordinators apply different models to some of the most challenging aspects of curriculum implementation that extend beyond the launch to help sustain curriculum implementation efforts. They coach and facilitate learning teams on how to shape lessons that address students' culture, context, race, and ethnicity. Mentoring and coaching on appropriate adaptation of lessons to meet the needs of students is key to ensuring the curriculum is applied appropriately.

This support equips teachers to scaffold lessons to connect less-prepared students with rigorous content and instructional materials. Scaffolding is a complicated concept, and while educative curriculum materials offer guidance, most teachers benefit from additional support that is sustained over several years of implementation. Many schools have professional learning community *time* allocated, and much of this work can be embedded in their learning cycles. One of the biggest barriers to successful curriculum implementation is often the unwillingness to commit and sustain the time required. Finding ways to demonstrate the value of time allocated to ongoing curriculum-based professional learning is key to maintaining momentum and support.

Putting Essential
Elements **Into Action**

- Support *leadership* at all levels in the organization to articulate and amplify the shared vision for teaching and learning that addresses each subject or grade level and the role of curriculum-based professional learning.

- Secure opportunities to protect and extend *resources* through partnerships, open education resources, and other funding sources.

- Promote instructional *coherence* by prioritizing and facilitating professional learning grounded in district curriculum and instructional materials.

Professional learning providers, curriculum developers, and district curriculum coordinators play unique roles in schools and systems concerning the Essential *Elements*. With limited authority but tasked with important responsibilities, these educators are the linchpin for successful curriculum-based professional learning. They "lead up" by helping leaders to develop, articulate, and amplify a shared vision for teaching and learning. Professional learning providers and curriculum coordinators are responsible for creating experiences that build internal *leadership* capacity among teacher leaders, coaches, and school leaders. They facilitate understanding and application with the educators charged with implementing the vision. Through curriculum-based professional learning, professional learning providers and curriculum developers make the vision come alive using instructional materials for each grade and subject. Recognizing the limitation of *resources*, district curriculum coordinators are creative in identifying and extending resources through partnerships, open education resources, and other outside funding sources. Professional learning providers, curriculum developers, and district curriculum coordinators understand probably more than anyone in the system the importance of *coherence* of instructional plans. They use that understanding during curriculum selection, adoption, and implementation planning processes as well as throughout the execution of curriculum-based professional learning.

Reflect on this:

1. Which *Elements* are most critical for professional learning providers, curriculum developers, and district curriculum coordinators?

2. How are these educators identified, prepared, developed, and assessed for their roles and responsibilities in relation to the *Elements*?

3. What are key issues to consider for their professional learning?

Roles and Responsibilities

System and School Leaders

The final group we address is system and school leaders. Superintendents, assistant superintendents, directors (for our colleagues in nations other than the United States), principals, and assistant principals implement the *Elements* through the vision they advance, the leadership they exercise, and the allocation of resources necessary for effective execution. Through the various leadership roles and responsibilities including chief executive, supervisor, mentor, colleague, and learner, this group of educators has unique opportunities to advance successful implementation of the *Elements*, accelerating their impact across classrooms and schools. Many of the responsibilities they hold must be adapted for their local context and the different phases of curriculum selection, adoption, and implementation.

Many others contribute to the successful acceptance and implementation of curriculum-based professional learning. Most importantly, they include the institutions that oversee the preparation of our nations' teachers as well as the school boards, state and provincial education agencies, and legislators that set the legal parameters for student and teacher learning. While these roles are not addressed in this section, they influence the contexts in which the *Elements* thrive. Perhaps they are the subject of future books on this subject.

Putting Core Design
Elements Into Action

- Develop and promote a shared vision for teaching and learning that addresses each subject, the *curriculum*, and the role of curriculum-based professional learning in supporting that vision.

- Build the capacity of formal and informal leaders at all levels to promote *transformative learning*.

- Adopt policies and practices that prioritize access to high-quality curriculum materials, curriculum-based professional learning, and *equitable* outcomes for learners.

First and foremost, curriculum selection, adoption, and implementation should be driven by a clear and compelling instructional vision and instructional materials that lay out plans for achieving it in classrooms. Then ensure that all teachers have access to them. Access to high-quality instructional materials and curriculum-based professional learning is not an individual option. Rather, it is a district responsibility if *equity* and student success are priorities. The intended impact of high-quality instructional materials requires investments in curriculum-based professional learning to ensure effective implementation. Leaders at all levels recognize their responsibility for understanding the *curriculum* at a level that enables them to make appropriate decisions and support educators responsible for implementation. Well-prepared and skillful facilitators are essential to designing curriculum-based professional learning that results in *transformative learning* and positions learners to examine beliefs and assumptions. Require curriculum-based professional learning, in both its design and facilitation, to be grounded in the use of high-quality instructional materials, to deepen teachers' content knowledge, and to prepare educators to teach curriculum in a culturally responsive manner to increase success with all students.

Putting Functional Design *Elements* Into Action

- Develop professional learning designers, facilitators, and coaches who can apply *learning designs* that resemble those teachers will use with students.

- Expect curriculum-based professional learning to challenge *beliefs* and assumptions, mirror the instructional approaches students will experience, and promote reflection.

- Establish *reflection and feedback* cycles to assess the overall progress of the investment in curriculum-based professional learning and determine where improvements can be made.

- Adopt a *change management* plan that identifies key phases of curriculum implementation and the supports required during each.

System and school leaders can begin with the expectation that the Functional Design *Elements* are addressed in all system-wide professional learning. Ongoing professional learning for those responsible for designing and facilitating curriculum-based professional learning is one key to success. Effective *learning designs* for these leaders are anchored in the curriculum teachers are expected to use with students and mirror the instructional approaches students experience. In addition, effective curriculum-based professional learning challenges *beliefs* and assumptions about learning and teaching. System and school leaders support *reflection and feedback* cycles for educators at all levels, including themselves, engaged in or supporting curriculum implementation. These cycles are key to assessing the progress of the investment in effective curriculum implementation and identifying appropriate interventions to address challenges and maintain momentum. Successful curriculum implementation is guided by a *change management* plan that identifies key phases of curriculum implementation and the supports required during each. Engage representatives of all stakeholders in the development of the plan, commit to regular monitoring and reporting, and provide the essential resources to secure completion. System and school leaders deploy professional learning designers, facilitators, and coaches to develop and use change management tools to support successful curriculum implementation. Consider partnering with curriculum and professional learning experts to develop tools that support specific curricula.

Putting Structural
Design *Elements*
Into Action

- Identify and develop professional learning designers, facilitators, and coaches who are committed to *collective participation* with expertise in content and curriculum and can facilitate collaborative learning.

- Ensure evidence and research inform the criteria and selection for *models* of professional learning applied throughout the different phases of curriculum implementation.

- Audit and prioritize resources, including *time* for curriculum-based professional learning.

System and school leaders advocate for *collective participation* and the power of shared responsibility for the success of all students. Collaborative learning structures and the time to implement them effectively are recognized as essential if the benefit of collective participation is to be realized. While system and school leaders rarely are the designers, facilitators, and coaches for curriculum-based professional learning, we recognize that some of their most important contributions are hiring and developing those with expertise in content and curriculum, as well as designing and facilitating collaborative learning. Designing and executing curriculum-based professional learning is more challenging than traditional "sit and get" workshops. Having the right people with the appropriate knowledge and skills is essential to its success.

System and school leaders ensure that criteria are established to ensure appropriate *models* of professional learning are used to get intended results and establish systems for monitoring the use of the criteria. They ensure change management plans include both high-level scheduling for individuals and groups of teachers and coaches, as well as the curriculum calendars and pacing guides that support day-to-day decisions by teachers and coaches. These leaders make public the calendars and pacing guides that document the support, materials, and time to be allocated to curriculum implementation.

They demonstrate their commitment by engaging in sessions designed for leaders and teachers and sharing personal reflections. Attending curriculum-based professional learning sessions demonstrates a commitment as well as provides opportunities to learn firsthand whether system and school expectations are being met. One payoff of effective curriculum-based professional learning is an increasing demand for more *time* and support. Having systems in place that include regular auditing of time and other resources provides information essential to determining whether and how additional time and support can be found.

Putting Essential *Elements* Into Action

- Build the capacity of formal and informal *leaders* at all levels to support curriculum-based professional learning.

- Allocate necessary *resources* with multiyear support for the implementation of high-quality instructional materials.

- Adopt policies and practices that promote (and eliminate those that inhibit) *coherent* systems of support for curriculum implementation.

The Essential *Elements* are the primary responsibility of system and school leaders. They are the foundation for the success of the combined *Elements*. System and school leaders have the authority and responsibility for the success of curriculum-based professional learning. *Leadership* is demonstrated through the execution of collaborative and representative processes used to develop the instructional vision and a comprehensive plan for realizing it. This comprehensive plan represents a multiyear effort that merits substantive *resources* throughout the process. While resources are always scarce, the budgeting and allocation processes demonstrate the priority placed on securing and implementing high-quality instructional materials in all classrooms and providing teachers with effective support for implementation. The COVID-19 pandemic gave leaders the opportunity to reexamine the significance of *coherence* in establishing a vision for instruction and their actions accordingly and avoiding previous tendencies toward "this year's new thing." Leaders are resolute in their commitment to stay the course.

Reflect on this:

1. Which *Elements* are most critical for system and school leaders?

2. How are the *Elements* embedded in the expectations for leaders?

3. What have been strengths and challenges to date regarding the *Elements*?

Closing Thoughts

Much has been written about the impact of the COVID-19 pandemic on society and education. Although it may seem contradictory to focus on opportunities, there has been some learning worthy of attention. For example, while conventional wisdom teaches us that substantive change takes years to plan, coordinate, and sustain, we learned that when faced with an emergency we can make new plans seemingly overnight. Imagine how history books may someday portray how millions of children went from attending school in-person to online in what could be characterized as a "flip of the switch." In that same vein, support for teachers transitioned from on-site workshops and coaching to tech-enabled online approaches.

Before and throughout the pandemic, educators focused on the selection and implementation of high-quality instructional materials and the support teachers needed for implementing them successfully. As we move beyond the pandemic, we hope greater attention will be given to curriculum-based professional learning and the issues we have highlighted.

We think the research and evidence base are compelling and point to the incredible opportunities offered students when their teachers leverage high-quality instructional materials in their classrooms. Yet, there are still forces that distract educators from this important work. The magnitude of change delineated in the *Elements* requires leadership from stakeholders at all levels. Educators working at both the school and system levels will serve their students best when they coalesce around a shared vision for instruction in the classroom, provide access to curriculum materials that advance that vision, and extend the ongoing support necessary to implement them successfully. Comprehensive change of this nature is difficult to launch and even more challenging to sustain. We hope the stories, observations, and suggested actions in this book inspire, inform, and sustain your efforts to improve curriculum-based professional learning.

Where do you go from here?

- Which direction will you take with information shared in this chapter?

- With whom will you share current reflections and actions you are considering?

- Is there additional learning you will pursue?

- What are the actions you will take in a week? A month? Six months?

- What are results you hope to report on at the end of the year?

The field of curriculum-based professional learning is still emerging. We are excited about the growing number of schools and systems that are prioritizing the adoption and implementation of high-quality instructional materials. Many of them are working with technical assistance partners to provide teachers with curriculum-based professional learning experiences that align with the *Elements* framework. We hope the framework and resources we have shared continue to support these efforts and entice others to engage in this work too. We invite readers to share with us your observations and new examples of the *Elements* in action. We want to hear what you are learning and any advice to the field.

This work is not easy and there are no quick fixes. Rigorous, inquiry-based teaching and learning require shifts in habits and knowledge and substantial changes in instructional practices and priorities. We offer the *Elements of curriculum-based professional learning* as both a guide and a call to action. Teachers deserve the highest quality professional learning to transform teaching and improve student learning.

References

MMMMMMMMMMMMMMMMMMMMMMMMMMMMMMMMMMM

Introduction

1. Isaac M. Opper, *Teachers Matter: Understanding Teachers' Impact on Student Achievement* (Santa Monica, CA: RAND Corporation, 2019), https://www.rand.org/pubs/research_reports/RR4312.html; Steven Cantrell and Thomas J. Kane, *Ensuring Fair and Reliable Measures of Effective Teaching: Culminating Findings from the MET Project's Three-Year Study* (Seattle: Bill & Melinda Gates Foundation, Policy and Practice Brief, Measures of Effective Teaching Project, January 2013).

2. David K. Cohen and Heather C. Hill, "Instructional Policy and Classroom Performance: The Mathematics Reform in California," *Teachers College Record* 102 (2000): 296–345; Geoffrey Saxe, Maryl Gearhart, and Na'ilah Nasir, "Enhancing Students' Understanding of Mathematics: A Study of Three Contrasting Approaches to Professional Support," *Journal of Mathematics Teacher Education* 4 (2001): 55–79, 10.1023/A:1009935100676; Jeremy Roschelle, Nicole Shechtman, Deborah Gail Tatar, Stephen Hegedus, Bill Hopkins, Susan Empson, Jennifer Knudsen, and Lawrence Paul Gallagher, "Integration of Technology, Curriculum, and Professional Development for Advancing Middle School Mathematics: Three Large-Scale Studies," *American Educational Research Journal* 47, no. 4 (2010): 833–878; Joseph A. Taylor, Stephen R. Getty, Susan M. Kowalski, Christopher D. Wilson, Janet Carlson, and Pamela Van Scotter, "An Efficacy Trial of Research-Based Curriculum Materials With Curriculum-Based Professional Development," *American Educational Research Journal* 52, no. 5 (2015): 984–1017, https://doi.org/10.3102/0002831215585962.

3. Ronald D. Anderson, "Curriculum Reform: Dilemmas and Promise," *Phi Delta Kappan* 77, no. 1 (1995): 33–36, http://www.jstor.org/stable/20405482.

4. Jim Short and Stephanie Hirsh, *The Elements: Transforming Teaching Through Curriculum-Based Professional Learning* (New York: Carnegie Corporation of New York, 2020), www.carnegie.org/elements.

5. Linda Darling-Hammond and Adam Edgerton, "Reinvention in Recovery," *Principal* 100, no. 1 (September/October 2021), https://www.naesp.org/resource/reinvention-in-recovery/.

6. Elizabeth Chu, Andrea Clay, and Grace McCarty, *Fundamental 4: Pandemic Learning Reveals the Value of High-Quality Instructional Materials to Educator-Family-Student Partnerships* (New York: Center for Public Research and Leadership at Columbia University, 2021).

7. TNTP, *The Mirage: Confronting the Hard Truth About Our Quest for Teacher Development* (New York: TNTP, 2015).

8. Linda Darling-Hammond, Maria E. Hyler, and Madelyn Gardner, *Effective Teacher Professional Development* (Palo Alto, CA: Learning Policy Institute, 2017).

9. Ruth Chung Wei, Linda Darling-Hammond, Alethea Andree, Nikole Richardson, and Stelios Orphanos, *Professional Learning in the Learning Profession: A Status Report on Teacher Development in the United States and Abroad* (Dallas, TX: National Staff Development Council, 2009).

10. Julia H. Kaufman, Katie Tosh, and Teryn Mattox, *Are U.S. Teachers Using*

High-Quality Instructional Materials? (Santa Monica, CA: RAND Corporation, 2020).

11. Andrea Prado Tuma, Sy Doan, Rebecca Ann Lawrence, Daniella Henry, Julia H. Kaufman, Claude Messan Setodji, David Grant, and Christopher J. Young, *American Instructional Resources Survey: 2019 Technical Documentation and Survey Results* (Santa Monica, CA: RAND Corporation, 2020).

12. Matthew M. Chingos and Grover J. "Russ" Whitehurst, *Choosing Blindly: Instructional Materials, Teacher Effectiveness, and the Common Core* (Washington, DC: Brookings Institute, 2012).

13. C. Kirabo Jackson and Alexey Makarin, *Can Online Off-the-Shelf Lessons Improve Student Outcomes? Evidence From a Field Experiment* (Cambridge, MA: National Bureau of Economic Research, 2017).

Chapter 1

1. Bill & Melinda Gates Foundation, *Teachers Know Best: Teachers' Views on Professional Development* (Seattle: Bill & Melinda Gates Foundation, 2015).

2. TNTP, *The Mirage: Confronting the Hard Truth About Our Quest for Teacher Development* (New York: TNTP, 2015).

3. Linda Darling-Hammond, Maria E. Hyler, and Madelyn Gardner, *Effective Teacher Professional Development* (Palo Alto, CA: Learning Policy Institute, 2017).

4. Bill & Melinda Gates Foundation, *Teachers Know Best: Teachers' Views on Professional Development* (Seattle: Bill & Melinda Gates Foundation, 2015).; TNTP, *The Mirage: Confronting the Hard Truth About Our Quest for Teacher Development* (New York: TNTP, 2015).

5. Ruth Chung Wei, Linda Darling-Hammond, Alethea Andree, Nikole Richardson, and Stelios Orphanos, *Professional Learning in the Learning Profession: A Status Report on Teacher Development in the United States and Abroad* (Dallas, TX: National Staff Development Council, 2009).

6. Bill & Melinda Gates Foundation, *Teachers Know Best: Teachers' Views on Professional Development* (Seattle: Bill & Melinda Gates Foundation, 2015).; TNTP, *The Mirage: Confronting the Hard Truth About Our Quest for Teacher Development* (New York: TNTP, 2015).

7. Scholastic, *Teacher and Principal School Report: Equity in Education* (New York: Scholastic, 2016).

8. Rivet Education, *2022 Trends in High-Quality Professional Learning* (Baton Rouge, LA: Rivet Education, 2022), https://riveteducation.org/wp-content/uploads/2022/04/2022-Trends-in-HQPL-Market-Report.pdf.

9. Julia H. Kaufman, Katie Tosh, and Teryn Mattox, *Are U.S. Teachers Using High-Quality Instructional Materials?* (Santa Monica, CA: RAND Corporation, 2020).

10. Horizon Research, *Highlights From the 2018 NSSME+* (Chapel Hill, NC: Horizon Research, 2019).

11. Andrea Prado Tuma, Sy Doan, Rebecca Ann Lawrence, Daniella Henry, Julia H. Kaufman, Claude Messan Setodji, David Grant, and Christopher J. Young, *American Instructional Resources Survey: 2019 Technical Documentation and Survey Results* (RAND Corporation, 2020).

12. Julia H. Kaufman, Sy Doan, Maria-Paz Fernandez, *The Rise of Standards-Aligned Instructional Materials for U.S. K–12 Mathematics and English Language Arts Instruction: Findings from the 2021 American Instructional Resources Survey.* (Santa, Monica, CA: RAND Corporation, 2022).

13. Sonja Brookins Santelises and Joan Dabrowski, *Checking In: Do Classroom Assignments Reflect Today's Higher Standards?* (Washington, D.C.: The Education Trust, September 2015). https://edtrust.org/resource/classroomassignments/; Keith, Dysarz, *Checking In: Are Math Assignments Measuring Up?* (Washington, D.C.: The Education Trust, April, 2018). https://edtrust.org/wp-content/uploads/2014/09/

CheckingIn_MATH-ANALYSIS_FINAL_5 .pdf; TNTP, *The Opportunity Myth* (New York: TNTP, 2018).

14. For example, see Cory Koedel and Morgan Polikoff, *Big Bang for Just a Few Bucks: The Impact of Math Textbooks in California* (Washington, DC: Brookings Institution, 2020); Rachana Bhatt, Cory Koedel, and Douglas Lehmann, "Is Curriculum Quality Uniform? Evidence From Florida," *Economics of Education Review* 34 (June 2013): 107–121.

15. Matthew M. Chingos and Grover J. "Russ" Whitehurst, *Choosing Blindly: Instructional Materials, Teacher Effectiveness, and the Common Core* (Washington, DC: Brookings Institution, 2012).

16. C. Kirabo Jackson and Alexey Makarin, *Can Online Off-the-Shelf Lessons Improve Student Outcomes? Evidence From a Field Experiment* (Cambridge, MA: National Bureau of Economic Research, 2017).

Chapter 2

1. Katherine L. McNeill, Renee Affolter, and Michael Clinchot, "Shifting From Learning About to Figuring Out," *Science Scope* (November/December 2021): 12–19, https://www.nsta.org/science-scope/ science-scope-novemberdecember-2021/ shifting-learning-about-figuring-out.

Chapter 3

1. Learning Forward, *Standards for Professional Learning* (Oxford, OH: Learning Forward, 2022).

2. Elizabeth Chu, Andrea Clay, and Grace McCarty, *Fundamental 4: Pandemic Learning Reveals the Value of High-Quality Instructional Materials to Educator-Family-Student Partnerships* (New York: Center for Public Research and Leadership at Columbia University, September 2021).

Chapter 4

1. Richard F. Elmore, *Bridging the Gap Between Standards and Achievement*
(Washington, DC: Albert Shanker Institute, 2002).

2. Elizabeth A. Davis and Joseph S. Krajcik, "Designing Educative Curriculum Materials to Promote Teacher Learning," *Educational Researcher* 34, no. 3 (April 2005): 3–14.

3. David Steiner, "Staying on the Shelf: Why Rigorous New Curricula Aren't Being Used," *Flypaper* (Fordham Institute, 2019), https://fordhaminstitute.org/national/ commentary/staying-shelf-why-rigorous- new-curricula-arent-being-used.

4. David Steiner, *Curriculum Literacy in Schools of Education? The Hole at the Center of American Teacher Preparation* (Johns Hopkins Institutes and Learning First, 2018), https://learningfirst.com/ wp-content/uploads/2020/07/8.-Curricu lum-literacy-in-schools-of-education.pdf.

5. Ibid.

6. C. Kirabo Jackson and Alexey Makarin, *Can Online Off-the-Shelf Lessons Improve Student Outcomes? Evidence From a Field Experiment* (Cambridge, MA: National Bureau of Economic Research, 2017).

7. Diane J. Briars and Lauren B. Resnick, *Standards Assessments—and What Else? The Essential Elements of Standards-Based School Improvement* (Los Angeles: National Center for Research on Evaluation, Standards, and Student Testing, 2000); Okhee Lee, Rachael Deaktor, Craig Enders, and Julia Lambert, "Impact of a Multiyear Professional Development Intervention on Science Achievement of Culturally and Linguistically Diverse Elementary Students," *Journal of Research in Science Teaching* 45, no. 6 (June 2008): 726–747; Sharon Lynch, Joel Kuipers, Curtis Pyke, and Michael Szcsze, "Examining the Effects of a Highly Rated Science Curriculum Unit on Diverse Students: Results From a Planning Grant," *Journal of Research in Science Teaching* 42, no. 8 (June 2005): 921–946; Rebecca M. Schneider and Joseph Krajcik, "Supporting Science Teacher Learning: The Role of Educative Science Materials," *Journal of Science Teacher Education* 13, no. 3 (2002): 221–245; Joseph A. Taylor, Stephen R. Getty,

Susan M. Kowalski, Christopher D. Wilson, Janet Carlson, and Pamela Van Scotter, "An Efficacy Trial of Research-Based Curriculum Materials With Curriculum-Based Professional Development," *American Educational Research Journal* 52, no. 5 (October 2015): 984–1017; Rachana Bhatt and Cory Koedel, "Large-Scale Evaluations of Curricular Effectiveness: The Case of Elementary Mathematics in Indiana," *Educational Evaluation and Policy Analysis* 34, no. 4 (December 2012): 391–412; Alana Bjorklund-Young, *High-Quality Curricula: A Cost-Effective Way to Boost Student Learning* (Baltimore: Johns Hopkins University School of Education, Institute for Education Policy, 2016).

8. Rodger W. Bybee, Joseph A. Taylor, April Gardner, Pamela Van Scotter, Janet Carlson Powell, Anne Westbrook, and Nancy Landes, *The BSCS 5E Instructional Model: Origins, Effectiveness, and Applications* (Colorado Springs: BSCS, 2006).

9. Brian J. Reiser, Michael Novak, Tara A. W. McGill, and William R. Penuel, "Storyline Units: An Instructional Model to Support Coherence From the Students' Perspective," *Journal of Science Teacher Education* 32, no. 7 (2021): 805–829.

10. David K. Cohen, Stephen W. Raudenbush, and Deborah Loewenberg Ball, "Resources, Instruction, and Research," *Education Evaluation and Policy Analysis* 25, no. 2 (June 2003): 1–24; Elizabeth A. Davis and Joseph S. Krajcik, "Designing Educative Curriculum Materials to Promote Teacher Learning," *Educational Researcher* 34, no. 3 (April 2005): 3–14; C. Kirabo Jackson and Alexey Makarin, *Can Online Off-the-Shelf Lessons Improve Student Outcomes? Evidence From a Field Experiment* (Cambridge, MA: National Bureau of Economic Research, 2017); Thomas J. Kane, Antoniya M. Owens, William H. Marinell, Daniel R. C. Thal, and Douglas O. Staiger, *Teaching Higher: Educators' Perspectives on Common Core Implementation* (Cambridge, MA: Harvard University, Center for Education Policy Research, 2016); Katherine L. McNeill,

"Teachers' Use of Curriculum to Support Students in Writing Scientific Arguments to Explain Phenomena," *Science Education* 93, no. 2 (August 2008): 233–268; David Steiner, "Materials Matter: Instructional Materials + Professional Learning = Student Achievement," *The Learning Professional* 39, no. 6 (December 2018): 24–28.

11. Charles L. Thompson and John S. Zeuli, "The Frame and the Tapestry: Standards-Based Reform and Professional Development," in *Teaching as the Learning Profession: Handbook of Policy and Practice*, ed. Linda Darling-Hammond and Gary Sykes (San Francisco: Jossey-Bass, 1999), 341–375.

12. Thomas R. Guskey, "Staff Development and the Process of Teacher Change," *Educational Researcher* 15, no. 5 (May 1986): 5–12.

13. Zaretta Hammond, *Culturally Responsive Teaching and the Brain* (Thousand Oaks, CA: Corwin, 2015).

14. Ibid., 15.

15. TNTP, *The Opportunity Myth* (New York: TNTP, 2018).

16. Hester De Boer, Anneke C. Timmermans, and Margaretha P. C. van der Werf, "The Effects of Teacher Expectation Interventions on Teachers' Expectations and Student Achievement: Narrative Review and Meta-analysis," *Educational Research and Evaluation* 24, no. 3–5 (December 2018): 180–200.

17. Lev S. Vygotsky, *Mind and Society: The Development of Higher Mental Processes* (Cambridge, MA: Harvard University Press, 1978).

18. Brad Emerling, James Hiebert, and Ron Gallimore, "Beyond Growth Mindset: Creating Classroom Opportunities for Meaningful Struggle," *Education Week Teacher*, December 7, 2015, https://www.edweek.org/tm/articles/2015/12/07/beyond-growth-mindset-creating-classroom-opportunities-for.html.

19. Zaretta Hammond, *Culturally Responsive Teaching and the Brain* (Thousand Oaks, CA: Corwin, 2015).

20. Debora L. Roorda, Helma M. Y. Koomen, Jantine L. Split, and Frans J. Oort, "The

Influence of Affective Teacher–Student Relationships on Students' School Engagement and Achievement: A Meta-analytic Approach," *Review of Education Research* 81, no. 4 (December 2011): 493–529.

21. Student Achievement Partners, *Instructional Practice Guide* (New York: Student Achievement Partners, 2018), https://achievethecore.org/page/1119/instructional-practice-guide.

22. Elizabeth Chu, Andrea Clay, and Grace McCarty, *Fundamental 4: Pandemic Learning Reveals the Value of High-Quality Instructional Materials to Educator-Family-Student Partnerships* (New York: Center for Public Research and Leadership at Columbia University (September 2021), 4.

Chapter 5

1. Michael G. Fullan, *The New Meaning of Educational Change*, 4th ed. (New York: Teachers College Press, 2007).

2. David Schleifer, Chloe Rinehart, and Tess Yanisch, *Teacher Collaboration in Perspective: A Guide to Research* (New York: Public Agenda, 2017).

3. Learning Forward and Stephanie Hirsh, "Focus Professional Learning Communities on Curriculum," *Education Week Teacher: Learning Forward PD Watch*, January 18, 2018, http://blogs.edweek.org/edweek/learning_forwards_pd_watch/2018/01/focus_professional_learning_communities_on_curriculum.html.

4. Susan Loucks-Horsley, Katherine E. Stiles, Susan Mundry, Nancy Love, and Peter W. Hewson, *Designing Professional Development for Teachers of Science and Mathematics*, 3rd ed. (Thousand Oaks, CA: Corwin, 2010).

5. Ibid.

6. For more about the impact of coaching on teacher and student performance, see Matthew A. Kraft, David Blazar, and Dylan Hogan, "The Effect of Teacher Coaching on Instruction and Achievement: A Meta-analysis of the Causal Evidence," *Review of Educational Research* 88, no. 4 (February 2018): 547–588.

7. Kwang Suk Yoon, Teresa Duncan, Silvia Wen-Yu Lee, Beth Scarloss, and Kathy L. Shapley, *Reviewing the Evidence on How Teacher Professional Development Affects Student Achievement* (Washington, DC: U.S. Department of Education, Institute of Education Sciences, National Center for Education Evaluation and Regional Assistance, Regional Educational Laboratory Southwest, 2007).

8. Linda Darling-Hammond, Maria E. Hyler, and Madelyn Gardner, *Effective Teacher Professional Development* (Palo Alto, CA: Learning Policy Institute, 2017).

9. Organisation for Economic Co-operation and Development, "Indicator D4," in *Education at a Glance 2014: OECD Indicators* (Paris: OECD Publishing, 2014), 474.

10. Holly Kuzmich, *Reimagining School: Rethink the School Day and Year to Better Serve Students and Families* (Dallas, TX: George W. Bush Institute, January 2021).

11. Learning Forward, *The Path to Instructional Excellence and Equitable Outcomes* (Oxford, OH: Learning Forward, 2019); Ross Weiner and Susan Pimentel, *Practice What You Teach: Connecting Curriculum and Professional Learning in Schools* (Washington, DC: The Aspen Institute, 2017).

12. Jennifer Bland, *COVID-19 Challenges Catalyze Promising Shifts in Professional Learning* (Washington, DC: Learning Policy Institute, November 2021).

13. Linda Darling-Hammond, Lisa Flook, Abby Schachner, Steve Wojcikiewicz, Pamela Cantor, and David Osher, *Educator Learning to Enact the Science of Learning and Development* (Washington, DC: Learning Policy Institute, 2022).

Chapter 6

1. Learning Forward, *Standards for Professional Learning* (Oxford, OH: Learning Forward, 2022).

2. Linda Darling-Hammond, Maria E. Hyler, and Madelyn Gardner, *Effective Teacher*

Professional Development (Palo Alto, CA: Learning Policy Institute, 2017); Laura M. Desimone, "Improving Impact Studies of Teachers' Professional Development: Toward Better Conceptualizations and Measures," *Educational Researcher* 38, no. 3 (2009), 181–199.

3. Amanda Fuchs Miller and Lisette Partelow, *Successful Implementation of High-Quality Instructional Materials* (Washington, DC: Center for American Progress, 2018).

4. Zaretta Hammond, *Culturally Responsive Teaching and the Brain* (Thousand Oaks, CA: Corwin, 2015).

5. Research has surfaced tremendous guidance for designing learning experiences that transform beliefs. See, for example, Barbara Scott Nelson and James K. Hammerman, *Reconceptualizing Teaching: Moving Toward the Creation of Intellectual Communities of Students, Teachers and Teacher Educators* (Newton, MA: Center for Development of Teaching, Education Development Center, 1994); Deborah Loewenberg Ball and David K. Cohen, "Developing Practice, Developing Practitioners: Toward a Practice-Based Theory of Professional Development," in *Teaching as the Learning Profession: Handbook of Policy and Practice*, ed. Linda Darling-Hammond and Gary Sykes (San Francisco: Jossey-Bass, 1999), 3–32; Charles L. Thompson and John S. Zeuli, "The Frame and the Tapestry: Standards-Based Reform and Professional Development," in *Teaching as the Learning Profession: Handbook of Policy and Practice*, ed. Linda Darling-Hammond and Gary Sykes (San Francisco: Jossey-Bass, 1999), 341–375.

6. Prior research suggests the importance of linking activities that create cognitive dissonance with those that help teachers resolve it. See, for example, Michael Huberman, "Networks That Alter Teaching: Conceptualizations, Exchanges and Experiments," *Teachers and Teaching: Theory and Practice* 1, no. 2 (July 2006): 193–211; John Seely Brown, Allan Collins, and Paul Duguid, "Situated Cognition and the Culture of Learning," *Educational Researcher* 18, no. 1 (January–February

1989): 32–42; Deborah Loewenberg Ball and David K. Cohen, "Developing Practice, Developing Practitioners: Toward a Practice-Based Theory of Professional Development," in *Teaching as the Learning Profession: Handbook of Policy and Practice*, ed. Linda Darling-Hammond and Gary Sykes (San Francisco: Jossey-Bass, 1999), 3–32; Charles L. Thompson and John S. Zeuli, "The Frame and the Tapestry: Standards-Based Reform and Professional Development," in *Teaching as the Learning Profession: Handbook of Policy and Practice*, ed. Linda Darling-Hammond and Gary Sykes (San Francisco: Jossey-Bass, 1999), 341–375.

7. Steven G. Rivkin, Eric A. Hanushek, and John F. Kain, "Teachers, Schools, and Academic Achievement," *Econometrica* 73, no. 2 (March 2005): 417–458.

8. Stephanie Hirsh, Kay Psencik, and Frederick Brown, *Becoming a Learning System*, rev. ed. (Oxford, OH: Learning Forward, 2018).

9. Gene E. Hall and Shirley M. Hord, *Implementing Change: Patterns, Principles, and Potholes*, 3rd ed. (Boston: Allyn and Bacon, 2011).

10. Ibid.

11. Robert Evans, *The Human Side of Change: Reform, Resistance, and the Real-Life Problems of Innovation* (San Francisco: Jossey-Bass, 1996); Michael G. Fullan and Matthew B. Miles, "Getting Reform Right: What Works and What Doesn't," *Phi Delta Kappan* 73, no. 10 (June 1993): 745–752.

12. Linda Darling-Hammond and Milbrey W. McLaughlin, "Policies That Support Professional Development in an Era of Reform," *Phi Delta Kappan* 76, no. 8 (June 1995): 597–604.

13. Shirley M. Hord, Suzanne M. Stiegelbauer, Gene E. Hall, and Archie A. George, *Measuring Implementation in Schools: Innovation Configurations* (Austin, TX: Southwest Educational Development Laboratory, 2006).

14. Gene E. Hall, Archie A. George, and William L. Rutherford, *Measuring Stages of Concern About the Innovation: A Manual for Use of the SoC Questionnaire*

(Austin: The University of Texas at Austin, Research and Development Center for Teacher Education, 1977).

15. Susan F. Loucks, Beulah W. Newlove, and Gene E. Hall, *Measuring Levels of Use of the Innovation: A Manual for Trainers, Interviewers, and Raters* (Austin: The University of Texas at Austin, Research and Development Center for Teacher Education, 1975).

16. Susan Heck, Suzanne M. Stiegelbauer, Gene E. Hall, and Susan F. Loucks, *Measuring Innovation Configurations: Procedures and Applications* (Austin: The University of Texas at Austin, Research and Development Center for Teacher Education, 1981).

17. Michael G. Fullan, *The New Meaning of Educational Change*, 3rd ed. (New York: Teachers College Press, 2001).

Chapter 7

1. Stephanie Hirsh, Kay Psencik, and Frederick Brown, *Becoming a Learning System*, rev. ed. (Oxford, OH: Learning Forward, 2018).

2. Peter M. Senge, *The Fifth Discipline: The Art and Practice of the Learning Organization* (New York: Doubleday, 1994).

3. Linda Lambert, Deborah Walker, Diane P. Zimmerman, Joanne E. Cooper, Morgan Dale Lambert, Mary E. Gardner, and Margaret Szabo, eds., *The Constructivist Leader*, 2nd ed. (New York: Teachers College Press, 2002).

4. Peter M. Senge, *The Fifth Discipline: The Art and Practice of the Learning Organization* (New York: Doubleday, 1994).

5. Linda Lambert, "Toward a Deepened Theory of Constructivist Leadership," in *The Constructivist Leader*, 2nd ed., ed. Linda Lambert, Deborah Walker, Diane P. Zimmerman, Joanne E. Cooper, Morgan Dale Lambert, Mary E. Gardner, and Margaret Szabo (New York: Teachers College Press, 2002), 34–62.

6. Linda Lambert, "What Does Leadership Capacity Really Mean?," *Journal of Staff Development* 26, no. 2 (Spring 2005): 38–40.

7. Lindsey Tepe and Teresa Mooney, *Navigating the New Curriculum Landscape: How States Are Using and Sharing Open Educational Resources* (Washington, DC: Council of Chief State School Officers, 2018), 19.

8. Cory Koedel and Morgan Polikoff, *Big Bang for Just a Few Bucks: The Impact of Math Textbooks in California* (Washington, DC: Brookings Institution, 2020).

9. Learning Forward, *Standards for Professional Learning* (Oxford, OH: Learning Forward, 2011).

10. Holly Kuzmich, *Reimagining School: Rethink the School Day and Year to Better Serve Students and Families* (Dallas, TX: George W. Bush Institute, January 2021).

11. Susan Loucks-Horsley, Katherine E. Stiles, Susan Mundry, Nancy Love, and Peter W. Hewson, *Designing Professional Development for Teachers of Science and Mathematics*, 3rd ed. (Thousand Oaks, CA: Corwin, 2010).

12. EdReports, *The State of the Instructional Materials Market: 2021 Report*, Spring 2022, https://edreports.org/resources/article/2021-state-of-the-market.

13. Ibid.

14. Great Minds, "Frequently Asked Questions: What Is the Relationship Between EngageNY and Eureka Math?," https://greatminds.org/faq/what-is-the-relationship-between-engageny-and-eureka-math.

15. Julia H. Kaufman, Jill S. Cannon, Shelly Culbertson, Maggie Q. Hannan, Laura S. Hamilton, and Sophie Meyers, *Raising the Bar: Louisiana's Strategies for Improving Student Outcomes* (Santa Monica, CA: RAND Corporation, 2018).

16. EdReports, "EdReports Breaks New Ground With Inaugural Science Reviews," February 28, 2019, https://www.edreports.org/resources/article/edreports-breaks-new-ground-with-inaugural-science-reviews.

17. Morgan Polikoff, Elaine Lin Wang, Shira Korn Haderlein, Julia H. Kaufman, Ashley Woo, Daniel Silver, and V. Darleen Opfer, *Exploring Coherence in English Language Arts Instructional Systems in the Common Core Era* (Santa Monica, CA: RAND Corporation, 2020), https://www.rand

.org/pubs/research_reports/RRA279-1
.html.

18. Michael Fullan and Joanne Quinn, *Coherence: The Right Drivers in Action* (Thousand Oaks, CA: Corwin, 2015).

19. Ibid.

20. Helen Timperley, *The Power of Professional Learning* (Maidenhead, UK: McGraw-Hill Education, 2011).

21. Michael Fullan and Joanne Quinn, *Coherence: The Right Drivers in Action* (Thousand Oaks, CA: Corwin, 2015).

22. Elizabeth Chu, Andrea Clay, and Grace McCarty, *Fundamental 4: Pandemic Learning Reveals the Value of High-Quality Instructional Materials to Educator-Family-Student Partnerships* (New York: Center for Public Research and Leadership at Columbia University, 2021)

Chapter 8

1. Bill and Melinda Gates Foundation, *Teachers Know Best: Teachers' Views on Professional Development* (Seattle, WA: Bill and Melinda Gates Foundation, 2015).

2. C. Kirabo Jackson and Alexey Makarin, *Can Online Off-the-Shelf Lessons Improve Student Outcomes? Evidence From a Field Experiment* (Cambridge, MA: National Bureau of Economic Research, 2017).

Index

Solutions YOU WANT | Experts YOU TRUST | Results YOU NEED

INSTITUTES

Corwin Institutes provide regional and virtual events where educators collaborate with peers and learn from industry experts. Prepare to be recharged and motivated!

corwin.com/institutes

ON-SITE PROFESSIONAL LEARNING

Corwin on-site PD is delivered through high-energy keynotes, practical workshops, and custom coaching services designed to support knowledge development and implementation.

www.corwin.com/pd

VIRTUAL PROFESSIONAL LEARNING

Our virtual PD combines live expert facilitation with the flexibility of anytime, anywhere professional learning. See the power of intentionally designed virtual PD.

www.corwin.com/virtualworkshops

CORWIN ONLINE

Online learning designed to engage, inform, challenge, and inspire. Our courses offer practical, classroom-focused instruction that will meet your continuing education needs and enhance your practice.

www.corwinonline.com

PLSN209A8

Visit www.corwin.com

CORWIN

A SAGE Publishing Company

Helping educators make the greatest impact

CORWIN HAS ONE MISSION: to enhance education through intentional professional learning.

We build long-term relationships with our authors, educators, clients, and associations who partner with us to develop and continuously improve the best evidence-based practices that establish and support lifelong learning.

THE PROFESSIONAL LEARNING ASSOCIATION

Learning Forward is a nonprofit, international membership association of learning educators committed to one vision in K–12 education: Equity and excellence in teaching and learning. To realize that vision, Learning Forward pursues its mission to build the capacity of leaders to establish and sustain highly effective professional learning. Information about membership, services, and products is available from www.learningforward.org.